Not A Cabbage Rose

Jenny Rose

This book is dedicated to the Rest of the Bunch,
with special thanks to my better half,
without whom it would not have been possible.

All the happenings in this book are true,
but some of the names of the children have been changed.

© 1997 Jenny Rose

ISBN 1 85852 089 4

CONTENTS

FOREWORD

There have been lots of books written about triumph over adversity, and you might expect that this is yet another. But you would be wrong. True, it affirms faith and asks no awkward questions. However, there is a special quality to this story and I suspect it lies beyond anything that the author herself intended. The way I read it is as a remarkable illustration of a truth it took me half a lifetime to discover – namely that it is more blessed to receive than give.

Now don't get me wrong – this is a story told by someone who over the years has given unstintingly to some eighty-six children, most of them difficult to place because of behavioural or learning difficulties. She and her husband opened their home to them as foster parents, offered them their love and shared with them their family. She has had a caring career which has gone far beyond the call of duty. But the focus is not on what she's done.

The focus is on one amazing life from which she and everyone around received, grace upon grace, full measure, pressed down and overflowing. Of course it couldn't have happened if she hadn't taken this baby to her heart, expecting her to die within weeks. It couldn't have happened if she hadn't done the best she could for Claire, born with such severe spina bifida it was decided not to operate. But the fact that she simply enabled Claire to become herself and live a full life for twelve short years was rewarded with all the mutual love, enjoyment and commitment that makes a relationship into one of the most precious things of life.

By receiving from Claire, everyone around gave her dignity and respect. Friendship and reciprocity are what every person needs, not the kind of help, service, or patronising charity which fosters dependency. Instinctively this mother knew that. She tells her tale simply and unselfconsciously, a tale in which church life, faith and love just take their natural place, along with the determination to let Claire get dirty on the floor like any other kid at the crawling stage. And one begins to understand how saints are made in the ordinary . . . .

Frances Young

1

From small beginnings

'Hallo, Mrs Rose, we have a child for you, a hyperactive three year old called Matthew. We'll bring him tomorrow at three o'clock.'

That 'phone call sixteen years ago was the beginning of a whole new way of life.

I had worked as a teacher of biology and science in a nearby high school for five years, then left to start a family. Now our two girls were at school, and I felt the need to occupy myself with more than housework – not my first love! A good friend of ours had been fostering for years, and we had always taken an interest in her family's comings and goings; she asked why we didn't consider it for ourselves. We had a big house and garden, experience with children, and would be working at home. After an interval of thought when we veered between interest (yes, she's right) to panic (night feeds and nappies for ever – and what if . . . ?) the idea sat comfortably at the back of our minds, the interest gradually overcoming the panic. But we didn't take any action. Life was busy and we never got round to it. Anyway, how did one start?

Then one evening my husband Elvin bought the local paper on his way home from work (not a regular occurrence). An advertisement leapt out at us – 'Professional Foster Parents wanted'. We both felt it was right to apply, so we 'phoned for more details. They wanted a family who could take up to three children under five at a moment's notice, and also make assessments of a child's development and behaviour in a home

3

environment. For this an enhanced payment would be made over and above the standard fostering rate.

There was to be a meeting in a public hall for all interested in applying, where questions could be asked and more details given. This was a 'no strings' occasion; no commitment was implied by being there, so I arranged to go. At the meeting I listened with interest, but very quickly decided that there was no point in continuing with our application. There were at least thirty practising foster parents there, already approved and with proven track records behind them. Some were working for two or even three different Social Services departments, and spoke with an air of confidence and familiarity with the system which made me wonder why we, as complete novices, were even bothering to apply. This feeling was so strong that I 'phoned the next day to tell them not to continue with our application. The relevant social worker was out, but I was assured that the message would be passed on. It wasn't!

Out of the blue we had a 'phone call to make an appointment for a social worker to visit our home. She came in the daytime when I was alone, and just chatted. Then she came again in the evening to meet all of us, then to meet the girls without us. I never did find out what was said at that meeting – although we had nothing to hide you never know what children will come out with next, and they were only nine and seven. It couldn't have been too damning, though, as she kept on coming back! As we became more friendly with her over the months I dared to ask what had happened to the original thirty-odd applicants, and she told me they had been whittled down to ten, and then later it was three.

After about eight months of interviews, Elvin and I were invited to the head office to meet one of the Social Services bosses. We had a very long talk which started with him talking in terms of 'if' until we suddenly realised he was saying 'when'. We had got the job! Nothing was ever formally put in writing, but we went home quite torn with mixed emotions. On the one hand we were pleased at being chosen from so many apparently better-qualified, more experienced applicants; on the other hand we were terrified at what we'd let ourselves in for. There was no turning back now!

After all this, the next few weeks were a complete anticlimax. Nothing happened! No visits, no 'phone calls, no children. We had screwed our courage to face almost any challenge, and now life was just jogging along in its familiar routine. Then, almost exactly nine months after our first application, the 'phone rang. 'Hallo, Mrs Rose, we have a child for you, a hyperactive three year old called Matthew. We'll bring him tomorrow at three o'clock.'

So this was it. In at the deep end. And no garden gate to contain a hyperactive three year old! We did have a gate which deterred dogs from entering and docile children from leaving, but it would prove no obstacle to a child of this description. Our first job was a hasty visit to the local timber yard for a length of stout fencing and a solid gate, which was erected immediately, with the catch on the outside.

Matthew proved to be a blond charmer. He had an infectious grin and boundless energy linked with an enquiring mind, but we didn't find him hyperactive in the true sense of the word. He was intelligent and could concentrate well if you caught his interest; the trick was to keep new experiences coming so that he didn't have time to plot wickedness. He stayed exactly a year, then moved to a permanent placement.

During this first year there were others, coming and going. A three month old baby girl straight from hospital, suspected of being battered; a six year old who acted like a baby. Sleepless and without speech or play, her only activities were to perch on the back of an armchair when indoors, and, when outdoors, to scratch dirt out from between the paving stones and eat it. In all we had fourteen children that first year, and realised we had found our niche. Yes, it was hard work, but we found it so satisfying it didn't matter. Apart from seeing the children blossom in a peaceful, ordered, stimulating environment (their first experience of such a life for many) we also met so many interesting people: parents, social workers, other foster parents, adoptive families.

We had one baby of six weeks old. She came straight from the hospital where she had been born, and stayed with us while her adoptive family was organised. It was arranged that her new parents would meet her for the first time one Saturday morning at our house.

You can imagine that weekday mornings were very busy. The older girls had to be got to school, my husband to work, the baby (or babies) fed, everybody organised for the day and the kitchen tidied, so that I was ready to go to the shops for quite a large daily order. There were usually at least seven in the family, and they all had healthy appetites. Sundays weren't much better. We are both committed Christians, very active in our local church. I taught a morning Sunday School class, and the whole family always went to morning service; sometimes Elvin would be away taking the service at another church. The entire tribe had to be ready to roll by 10.15am, including any babies who expected a feed at 10am.

For these reasons we regarded Saturday as our 'day off', when the clock no longer ruled. The adoptive parents weren't due until 10, so we enjoyed our usual relaxed Saturday routine of breakfast in pyjamas, taking as long as we liked. Elvin opened the living room curtains at about 8am and remarked, 'There's a car outside.' It was the adoptive couple sitting in the half dark – it was November. We didn't find out how long they'd been there, but they had allowed plenty of time for the long and unfamiliar journey! Of course they came in and joined us for breakfast, fell in love with the baby, turned a blind eye to the general state of undress, and we all had a marvellous morning. They could hardly tear themselves away; the baby joined them about a week later.

We had several pre-adoption babies, and were thrilled to be present at the introductions. In each case the parents were overjoyed (and often overcome, both mums and dads). We supervised the first awkward feed and fumbling nappy change – this was still the era of pins and terry squares which had to be folded to fit. We heard the long story that had led up to this meeting, and told them what we could of their new baby's preferences and dislikes. Then came the sad moment when they had to leave the baby with us and go away until the formalities were completed, after which a social worker delivered the baby to their house.

Several families sent us photos of the baby at its christening or first birthday, and one even came to visit over five years later when she had started school and wanted to know more about her background. In each case we were struck by what a good job the adoption workers had done in physically matching the children with their new families. Not many of our children were adopted though; most went back home after the family crisis which brought them into care had been resolved, or at least smoothed over enough to allow the family to function again. We rarely heard anything of what became of them after they left us, and of course they were too young to be able to contact us themselves.

We soon became very aware of a young child's ability to live in the present, which helps them through some very unpleasant circumstances. Even if children's home lives are unsatisfactory from the outsider's point of view, it is what they are used to. Suddenly they are removed from it, usually taken for a medical check-up, then delivered to complete strangers and left. Most of them arrived totally bewildered, and with the best will in the world you can't give reasons and explanations to a very young child.

We found the best way to handle these children was to carry on round them as usual, including them when they were willing, and letting them be observers when they weren't. In a day or two they all joined in with whatever was going on. There were always other children about, which helped – the house was rather like a permanent small playgroup. I was always delighted when I heard a child humming or singing to itself when absorbed in play – a sure sign of contentment. Yet sometimes only a week or two before they had been caught up in situations which demanded their instant removal for their own safety. I never thought for a moment that they had forgotten any of this, but it seems to be that until a child develops a sense of time it lives only in the present. This is a great blessing for young children in times of stress, and carries them unscathed through situations which would cause great damage to an older child or an adult.

2

A sense of humour and a good washing machine

The Department of Employment runs periodical surveys of families all over the country, to gain figures for its statistics. The families are chosen at random and one year we found ourselves included. Husband and wife are interviewed separately, and mine took place in the garden one sunny afternoon. The official had a laptop computer with the forms already in it, and he only had to fill in my answers. After establishing who I was, where I lived and what I did, the next question was 'What qualifications do you need for this job?' I think he expected something like a degree, a set of GCSEs or a certificate to prove completion of a training course. My answer, without any need to think, was 'A sense of humour and a good washing machine.' He looked somewhat surprised!

When you have a houseful of children there are bound to be times when things don't run like clockwork. Even as simple a thing as a really rainy weekend can cause problems, and we found an ability to see the funny side of things very useful. Laughter is a great releaser of tension, and as we never had a day off, or any sick leave, there were times when we needed it. It wasn't only the children who sometimes caused us problems; some of the social workers did too. It is essential for a social worker to be able to drive, but one of them hadn't passed her test, so she had to come on the bus. We live almost in the country, half an hour's drive from the city our children came from, and not on a direct bus route. It took her a couple of hours to get here, and as she passed a chip shop she invariably bought a portion of curry and chips for her lunch, to have when she arrived. There are few foods we really dislike, but one of them is curry – both taste and smell. Every single time she came – and her child was with us for ten months – she would present me with a tray of cold, congealed, bright yellow chips and a request to warm it up for her. At that time we didn't have a microwave, so I had to stir it in a saucepan, inhaling the curry fumes and filling the house with noxious vapours. We didn't look forward to her visits!

My washing machine deserved a medal for service beyond the call of duty. Every single day it washed a load of clothes and then a load of nappies. Sometimes we had three children in nappies, and disposables were too expensive and not as good as they are now; we only used them for holidays. In addition there might be a third load of sheets if it was a good drying day or we had a bedwetter. I frequently ran out of line space, even with three long lines, but our neighbour let me use hers if it was free.

In addition to this routine washing, there was often an emergency load to do. Some children arrived with no clothes at all, while others had a plastic carrier bag hastily packed with an amazing assortment of garments. There was little regard for the size of the child or season of the year; apparently whatever was to hand was stuffed in regardless. There were often several different sizes, even adult clothes, and although clean they usually smelt strongly of cigarette smoke. They were always unpacked straight into the washing machine to get rid of the smell, which meant that some days four loads were done. One day Elvin came home from work and told me he'd ordered a tumble dryer. I was inclined to be horrified, as I'd heard that the running costs were astronomical, but it proved to be invaluable. Occasionally it was necessary to wash and dry a child's clothes overnight so they could be worn again the next day, and this would have been impossible without the dryer.

Ironing was always a problem, although I did as little as possible. Things like pyjamas and underwear were never ironed, and many things could be folded straight from the dryer.

This left mainly dresses and shirts, which mounted up alarmingly. I wouldn't use an iron with toddlers about, which meant that it had to be done at night, and by then I was usually tired.

The housework, too, was reduced to the bare minimum. It was much more enjoyable to play with the children, so the house never got what my grandmother called 'bottomed'. At first this didn't matter, but by the time we'd had thirty-one children (in nearly two years) I was getting very conscience-stricken about my inability to reach Ideal Home standards.

The solution to these problems arrived in the shape of 'Aunty Shirley'. This was the friend who had first introduced us to fostering, so she knew the ropes and handled the children beautifully. She also ironed, cleaned windows and pulled beds out, in fact she became known as my second pair of hands. She came for two mornings a week, which made a world of difference to my losing battle on the housekeeping front. As well as cleaning and ironing, Aunty Shirley made life much easier as I could leave her in charge while I went to the dentist; having a row of interested spectators doesn't add anything to the pleasures of dental attention! If I had to take one child to the doctor or the hospital she would look after the rest, which made things much easier, and she or I could dash to the shops for bread on a stormy day without having to get everybody wet. Her only complaint was the time it took to peg the washing out! Rows of socks and small garments went out every fine day, sometimes more than once if we had a shower; it often took a full half-hour to get it all on the line.

In the sixteen years since the first momentous 'phone call we have worn out only two washing machines, which I think is a credit to the manufacturer. We had a service contract and whenever the man came he always told me, 'It does 'em good to use 'em', but I don't think he ever realised quite how much we used 'em!

By the time we had fostered forty children (which took two and a half years) the routine was well established. There would be the usual, 'Hello, Mrs Rose, we have a child for you' 'phone call, or sometimes, just for variety, 'Hello, Mrs Rose, do you have a vacancy?' Very often Elvin would come home from work to find a new face at the tea table, and once I played a really sneaky trick on our two girls.

They had gone to Brownies one Wednesday evening as usual, and soon afterwards we were asked to take a four month old baby boy as an emergency. We already had one four month old baby boy, who had been bathed and dressed in a blue Babygro ready for bed, before Brownies. While the girls were away he was put to bed, and number two arrived. He was wearing an identical Babygro, so I put him on the floor on a blanket where the other baby had been earlier. They were of similar colouring, and when the girls returned from Brownies I didn't say anything. It took about an hour of sideways looks and puzzled scrutiny before I was asked, 'What have you done to Graham? He looks different!' When I explained they were quite thrilled, and next day played at having twins – we've always fancied some, but never had any.

The 'phone call for child number forty-two was different, however. We were asked to take a new-born baby girl with spina bifida, who was expected to die within six weeks. Usually the child in question arrived about half an hour after the social worker's call, but this time we needed to think about it. My first thought was what the effect might be on the other children, particularly our own two. By now they were quite accustomed to children coming and going, but dying was different. And what, exactly, was spina bifida? I had vaguely heard of it, but didn't really know what it meant, or how to look after anybody with it. We talked to the girls about it, and decided we would see the baby in hospital before we made our minds up. Since all the children would be affected if we decided to take her, we all went to visit the Special Care Baby Unit. As well as Elvin and me, there was Maggi, then thirteen; Liz, who was nearly eleven, Sarah (four), and Mark (three). We used up the whole row of white gowns on pegs outside the door!

It had been agreed that if anybody was frightened or repulsed by the baby's appearance, we would forget the whole idea. We had no idea what to expect, and had mentally braced ourselves for the worst. The nurse took us into a large room filled with what appeared to be plastic fish tanks. Each clear rectangular box held a tiny premature baby, not yet big enough to go home, but not needing intensive care any more.

The nurse led us over into a corner where there was a large full-term baby who looked like a stranded whale compared with her miniature companions! Like all the others she was lying on her side, wrapped shawl-style in a white blanket, and was asleep. She had a round face, a bit of dark blonde fluff instead of hair, invisible eyebrows and long lashes. Apart from her size, she looked like all the other babies there. Our nervousness evaporated instantly. Instead of being repelled, as we half expected, we all felt protective and loving, even the two little ones. The nurse picked her up and unwrapped her to show us her back, which had a large red bubble on it at waist level. It looked unpleasant but not horrific. The children reacted to it much as they would to a badly grazed knee.

They were clamouring to take her home with us there and then, but there were practical considerations to be taken into account. The first was her expected imminent death. I was afraid that meant she would just suddenly expire, but the nurse explained it would be a gradual deterioration over a few days or a week; there would be plenty of time to return her to the hospital. This seemed to put a little distance between the children and the event, and made it easier to handle. They had already fallen in love with her, and if her life was to be only short, they wanted to help to make it happy. After all, they had plenty of experience of being Big Sisters.

The second thing to consider was her nursing care. She needed handling differently from a normal baby, and her back had to be dressed twice a day with special sterile dressings. It was arranged that I would visit on my own to learn these special techniques.

The third consideration was one of space. All this happened in the middle of December, and we were due to have visitors for Christmas. My sister and her husband and two children lived abroad, and they were paying a visit to England. They were staying with us over Christmas and New Year, and with four of them and six of us the house would be full to bursting, with no extra room for even the tiniest baby!

The hospital agreed to keep her over Christmas, which gave me time to learn how to look after her. Her schoolgirl mum had already returned home to her widowed mother in Scotland. They lived in a small village where everybody knew everything, and once the pregnancy couldn't be concealed, the girl was sent to England to stay with her aunt and uncle. Arrangements had been made for the baby to be adopted at birth, and a couple had been identified as parents, but when the baby was born unexpectedly handicapped it all fell through. Special Care needed the cot for other babies – there was nothing they could do for her beyond maintenance –which was when Social Services rang us.

We found out that, generally speaking, spina bifida babies have their backs operated on within hours of birth. Spina bifida literally means 'split spine' – the bones of the back fork into two for part of their length, then go back together again further along. The gap where the split is allows the soft spinal cord to bulge out, instead of being safely encased in solid bone. All the nerves to the legs and lower part of the body are in the spinal cord, and the bulging damages them to a greater or lesser degree. Immediate operation limits further damage, and also the very great risk of infection, which can easily prove fatal. Spina bifida is very variable, ranging from a slight dimple in the skin, which has no effects at all, to complete 'boiling over' of the spinal cord which means no feeling or movement below that point. Claire's was the worst type. Her spinal cord was exposed and had no skin cover, only a polythene-like membrane which oozed clear fluid. In Claire's case, no operation was done because the spina bifida was so severe that she wasn't expected to live anyway, and her social background was taken into account. Her mother wasn't able to look after her, her grandmother was unsympathetic, and her prospective adoptive family couldn't be expected to take a baby only to have it die almost straight away.

So she came to us, and already we could see a change in her – her head had started to swell, especially the forehead. The 'soft spot' on top of her head was bigger than before, and the doctors told us this was hydrocephalus, or water on the brain, a condition commonly associated with spina bifida. As soon as this is detected another operation drains off the excess fluid by inserting a tube into the head and running it under the skin to the heart or abdomen, but the doctors didn't think it was worth doing in Claire's case; better to let her die peacefully without having to undergo the stress of surgery.

Claire arrived at our house on the 4th January, at exactly one month old. All she had to call her own was a soft pink jacket and a silver christening bracelet – her life expectancy was so short she had been christened at birth. We discovered that she had been fed on demand. At first we thought this meant when she was hungry rather than at standard three or four hourly intervals, but it actually meant that if the baby didn't cry, she wasn't fed. Babies on this system gradually became weaker and faded gently away, but Claire had other ideas! She demanded milk at regular intervals, and was actually gaining weight.

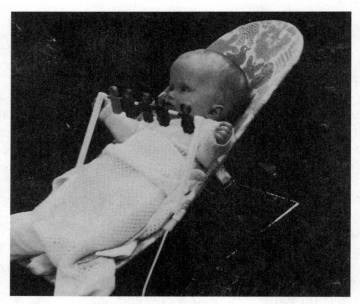

I had to take her back to the Special Care Unit twice a week so that they could keep an eye on her. Gradually the bump on her back healed over, not with skin but with a membrane – like parchment, thicker where it had been like polythene before, and transparent where it had been oozing. It stopped leaking, which greatly lessened the chance of infection, and she steadily gained weight. The six-week deadline passed, then two months, and she showed no sign of dying. The hospital visits reduced to once a week, then once a fortnight, and she still kept on going.

All this time her head had been expanding steadily. The 'soft spot' was now very large and not soft at all; it was hard and tense as the build up of pressure inside her brain forced the bones of her skull apart.

When it got to late February and she was still with us, she was admitted to hospital overnight for observation. Since she hadn't co-operated by dying, a decision had to be made about whether or not to operate. We took her in one morning and arranged to collect her the next, when the decision would have been made.

3

'Only a cabbage'

Elvin took half a day off work so that we could both go to the hospital, refreshed after our first night uninterrupted by feeds since the New Year. As we entered the ward we happened to meet the paediatrician just finishing his round, so he took us aside for a private chat. The only non-public place available was the cleaner's cubby-hole, so we sat surrounded by mops and buckets while he gave us his verdict.

He went over Claire's medical history to date, then told us bluntly what would happen next. He pulled no punches in explaining how her head would continue to swell; she would go blind, and suffer kidney failure; in the unlikely event that she lived she would only be a cabbage with no quality of life at all. For these reasons there was no point in operating to try to extend her life. He closed his file and stood up to indicate that the interview was over, advising us to take her home with us now, but adding that he didn't expect her to live beyond the age of six months. Dear Elvin just looked at him and said calmly that we believe God can heal, whereupon the doctor scuttled out like a rabbit!

We collected Claire, and as we drove home Elvin kept asking me what I was smiling at. I hadn't realised I was, but I had a strong and deep conviction, very difficult to put into words, that what we had just heard from the doctor was not going to happen.

We had booked an Easter holiday in a North Wales chalet that year, and Elvin took the opportunity to attend a local dinner meeting organised by Christian businessmen. He usually went to the one in our area, but had missed it due to being on holiday. The speaker was an American whose blocked heart valves had been dramatically cleared by God, and he now went about telling people what had happened and also prayed for those who needed healing. A friend of ours was chauffeuring him round, and as it was the Easter holidays his daughter came too. She stayed the night with us at the chalet rather than travel back to where they were staying, so her father and the American came the next morning to collect her.

I was a bit nervous of this American! I had heard that when he prayed for people they fell over backwards; in fact he had 'catchers' standing at the ready. This wasn't my style at all, and I was so afraid he might burst into prayer while they were there at the chalet that I wedged myself firmly into the corner of the settee, and held the baby as protection. Claire was now four months old and looked very odd with her huge head (bigger than mine) and tiny body. The two men came in and sat down while our visitor collected her things, and I could see the American looking at Claire. Eventually he asked about her, and Elvin told him what the doctor had said. He came over and gently placed one hand on her head as she lay in my arms, and prayed for her. To my great relief nothing apparently happened! They collected their passenger and left, and we continued with our holiday.

Over the next few weeks there were subtle changes in Claire. She began to watch what was going on around her, to respond to attention, and then to smile. It was as if she had fully woken up for the first time in her life. Monthly check-ups at the hospital showed that her head had stopped growing, and as it became obvious that she wasn't going to die, she was introduced to physiotherapy. She absolutely hated those sessions! Blue paper sheets were used for the children to lie on, and hers got so wet from her tears that they disintegrated within minutes. The physios were very gentle, but apparently she had a very low pain threshold and any large movements made to her arms or legs pulled on her back. One of the doctors told me that it was as sensitive to touch as an eye, so it was no wonder she cried.

Eventually Claire was sent to another department to have a plastic mould made for her back which would let me lie her face up, or could be leaned against cushions to raise her up a little. As she got more used to it I started to wedge it in a pushchair when in the reclined position so that she was nearly sitting up. This freed her hands for playing on a table, and she learnt to play with bricks and all the usual baby toys. By her first birthday she was saying Mum-um and Dad-ad, and playing almost normally. She was restricted by what she could reach and by the fact that she couldn't raise her head out of the mould – it was too heavy – but she was happy and responsive.

All this happened only at home though! Each time she saw a physio she went on strike. I would report small achievements or little bits of progress, and she would let me down every time. The staff gave me pitying looks, obviously thinking I was a fond doting mum who was just deluding myself. Then one week Claire suddenly decided to show off and went through her whole repertoire; the physio went and fetched all her colleagues to watch this amazing sight.

The doctors now decided to operate on her head to insert the shunt which would drain excess fluid from her brain. They were a bit late, as her head had long stopped growing! Measured around the back, just above her ears and across her forehead (they referred to it as 'measuring for a new hat') it had been a steady seventy-six centimetres for the last few check-ups.

Claire went into hospital at fifteen months old and was so interested in her new surroundings that she lifted her head up for the first time to have a better look. The physiotherapy was paying off at last! She had always lain on her tummy, and now pushed down on her hands to raise her head, then leaned on her elbows while she inspected her cubicle. The clown curtains met with her approval, and there were plenty of bright murals and motifs to catch her eye.

She had to have a brain scan before the operation, which meant a trip by ambulance to another hospital. It was essential that she lay still, so they gave her a sedative, but instead of sedating her it made her silly and giggly, and the nurse said she was drunk! She flirted outrageously with the ambulanceman who travelled with us, but fortunately it wasn't a long journey. When we got there, we encountered a problem – her head was too big to fit into the hole in the scanner. We hung about for a long time while various people were consulted, then they decided to dismantle the casing and so enlarge the hole. All this took ages, but at least it gave the sedative time to wear off. When we finally got her into position she was rather fed up, but it was still essential that she lay perfectly still. I had been singing nursery rhymes to her until I was hoarse, but kept going for a few more vital minutes while they took their pictures. Luckily she co-operated, and they only had to do it once.

Elvin took time off work to look after the rest of the children, and I commuted daily to the hospital, returning each night to put the others to bed after I had settled Claire. She was in for ten days and enjoyed her stay. Somebody else's toys are always more interesting than your own, and the ward had a well-stocked playroom. She wasn't old enough to mind that they had shaved one side of her head, although that, and the stitches, gave her a more peculiar appearance than ever.

Another department made her a special seat. This was the Orthotic Unit, which was new to me and absolutely fascinating. They positioned Claire comfortably on a big bean bag full of polystyrene beads, which didn't hurt her back as they punched a dent in it first. They kept adjusting it, and her, until she was in a good sitting position with the back of her head supported on a sort of shelf of beads, then sucked all the air out of the bag with an electric pump. The beads no longer had room to move, and became as solid as a rock. When I lifted Claire out there was a perfect replica of her shape which was then lined with plaster to make a model of her. This model would later be used when making the moulded seat; the air was let back into the bean bag and it was ready for use again. So simple, so effective, and with no inconvenience at all to Claire.

Some weeks later we went back to collect the finished product. They had mounted the seat on a small wheelchair frame, and of course the mould fitted her perfectly. She loved sitting up properly, and it also solved another problem. We spent a lot of time in the car going to hospital appointments, and I wasn't at all happy about her safety. When she was tiny she travelled in a carry-cot on the back seat, but she had long outgrown it. We couldn't use a toddler car seat as we did with our other children because it would hurt her back, so she had to lie face down along the back seat. This was less than satisfactory, but we could find no other solution. Now that we had the moulded seat there was no problem. I could lift Claire and the seat together off the frame, and put them as one into the car with the seat belt round to hold it all firm. She was much safer, and was delighted to be able to see out of the window. The only problem now was that we had to change the car! The wheelchair base wouldn't fit into the boot, so we had to sell our saloon and buy an estate.

The Orthotic Unit later made Claire a standing frame, which allowed her to investigate drawers and see the world from a different angle. By now she had some head control, and could keep her head up for longer and longer periods as she stood up to do things. She could also lift her head out of the seat mould to look down at her hands, which made doing everything a lot easier – before then she had to feel for a toy and then lift it up to eye level to see it. Eating was a lot less messy too, as she could now see what she was doing.

21

I worked hard at stimulating her, providing new experiences, and generally broadening her horizons. I found that I had an unsuspected talent for adaption, making possible activities that didn't seem available at first glance to anyone in a wheelchair.

My friends were always amused at the lengths to which I went to get Claire dirty! They seemed to spend all their time telling their toddlers to keep out of the dirt, especially the boys. When Claire was tiny I would sometimes lie her face down on a skateboard in the garden so that she could scrabble in the earth, mud or grass, and grab daisies. I always hoped that she would push herself along with her hands, the equivalent of crawling, but she had other ideas. Even at that age she had great determination and couldn't be forced into anything she didn't want to do!

I have since met quite a few handicapped children whose parents keep them clinically clean at all times. They always look nice, but I'm sure that sometimes a happy child is a grubby child, and they *are* washable!

It wasn't until Claire could sit unaided, when she was about two and a half, that she was able to have a bath. Until then I put her face down on the draining board, with her head towards the sink, on a towel so the metal didn't feel cold to her tummy. Her hair was washed one side at a time, and the whole process was rather tedious.

Before she could sit up I couldn't put her in the bath as one hand was needed to protect her back when semi-reclined, and one to support her head, which left me nothing to wash her with. As soon as she was promoted to the bath I only needed one hand available to steady her if necessary, and could wash her comfortably. It also gave Claire great opportunities to play with the water, which she enjoyed very much.

Progress was steady, and by the time Claire was three she was an accomplished conversationalist, played with all the usual toddler toys, and loved to bake and dabble with water, sand and paint. She had also developed an impish sense of humour. This cabbage was ready for playgroup!

The playgroup which Maggi and Liz had attended had no vacancies, so I approached the other one in our village. The board outside read 'Daily playgroup. Mornings. Please call in', so we did. They made an appointment for us to go for an hour the following week, and Claire played while I observed in the background. She fitted in with no problems; although she couldn't propel herself from one activity to another there were plenty of pushers. I was pleased with the way the other children accepted her, just like ours did at home, and Claire enjoyed the range of different toys.

When all the others went home we stayed for a few minutes to discuss arrangements, and the leader came to ask me questions. Her main concern was whether Claire could get out of her wheelchair to go to the toilet! I explained that she was doubly incontinent and still in nappies, and therefore wouldn't need to go to the toilet; and also that if she could get out of her wheelchair she wouldn't be in it in the first place, but it was no good. The leader refused to accept Claire because she wasn't toilet trained, and I went home feeling very frustrated. From Claire's earliest days she had met with only friendship and encouragement from all the adults in her life, whether at home, church or hospital, and I felt this uncompromising attitude was quite unreasonable. Claire was quite unaffected by it as she didn't understand what was going on, but my feathers were considerably ruffled.

Some months later another smaller playgroup opened, which accepted Claire without any fuss. Unfortunately it was too small to be economical and had to close within quite a short time, so we were back to square one. In the meantime Aunty Shirley had left me to my own devices and started to work in a shop. We had told Social Services that we wanted to keep Claire long term and the flow of children had lessened considerably. Once Claire had started playgroup I felt I had time to do the housework unaided, so when Aunty Shirley was offered another job she accepted it.

A young mum in our church ran a playgroup about three miles away so when the new playgroup closed I asked her if there were any vacancies and Claire started there at the beginning of the next term. As things turned out this was the best move she could have made as it affected all her subsequent education. God moves in mysterious ways!

This playgroup was held in a room within a primary school, and when the children became old enough they moved into the reception class in another part of the building almost without noticing it. They were used to seeing the teachers and older pupils, and visits into the main part of the school could be made very easily. To make matters even better from our point of view, it had been built very recently and had ramped doorways, no stairs, and even a disabled toilet.

Mums I met who had older children there were all very satisfied with the teaching and general atmosphere, and also it was one of the feeder primaries for an equally new and well-designed High School. Although this had some upstairs classrooms there was a lift, and its reputation was good and getting better.

Once Claire passed her fourth birthday the question of formal education was raised. We were invited to visit our nearest large town, where there was a primary school for the physically disabled children of the district. They made us very welcome and the staff were obviously totally dedicated, but Claire was unable to communicate with any of the other children. Many of them had cerebral palsy, and although they were bright enough they couldn't talk intelligibly. The lesson in progress was how to use a knife and fork, which Claire had already mastered, and we felt that she wouldn't be stretched enough. The real plus point was that all the children received daily physiotherapy, and we realised that we had to make a choice. Did we accept a place here and make the most of Claire's physical possibilities, or push for a place at an ordinary school and stimulate her mind at the expense of her body? We considered these alternatives very carefully and finally decided to apply for a place in the school where she already went to playgroup.

No amount of physio would make her legs work, and she had to take her place in the big wide world eventually, so we felt she may as well begin now, although life would no doubt be harder for her with ordinary children than in the sheltered environment of the special school.

A disabled child can't just be accepted at an ordinary school; there is a lengthy process called Statementing which has to be undergone first. This involves medicals, doctors' and psychologists' reports, and many forms to fill in. The headteacher had popped in to the playgroup to have an informal look at Claire (another advantage of sharing the same building) and had agreed in principle, and now we awaited the decision of the local education office.

We received copies of the various reports. Here is an extract from the one the educational psychologist wrote after visiting Claire at home:

> . . . . Claire obtained a score exactly on par for her age, giving a standardised score of 101. The Naming Vocabulary test yielded another score within the normal range, showing that as far as these aspects of receptive and expressive language are concerned Claire is functioning at her age level.
> It is evident therefore that Claire has normal language skills but her drawing skills are below average. She has no feeling below the waist, cannot use her legs and needs regular toileting. However, she is fully mobile in her wheelchair and has a delightful personality.

We also received a copy of letters written by her hospital doctors, and we were very gratified with one of them from the paediatrician who had told us she would only ever be a cabbage:

> Claire was born with spina bifida and hydrocephalus. Initially a decision was made not to intervene surgically but when it became apparent that Claire was developing encouragingly, a shunt was inserted to relieve the pressure of hydrocephalus.
> Claire, with the indefatigable efforts of her loving foster parents and associated health workers has made excellent developmental progress.
> Claire is a delightful girl who should be encouraged to attend normal school where I am confident she would contribute greatly.

Another letter spoke of 'remarkable progress, so that at the age of four years her understanding and expressive language are appropriate to her chronological age'.

We were very pleased with all these comments. Although we felt Claire had normal mental powers for her age it was nice to have it confirmed independently. I sometimes got the impression that I wasn't always believed when I told strangers what she could do. They expected her to be acutely handicapped and so took what I told them with several pinches of salt!

After months of reports and committee meetings, the Statement was completed. Claire was recommended for mainstream education, with a classroom helper provided to assist her when necessary. The school of our choice accepted her, and our miraculous little 'cabbage' was promoted from playgroup to reception class along with the rest of her friends.

4

No bumps

Although Claire's fifth birthday was just before Christmas, she started school the September before. She settled in quickly and coped without any problems. She was the only wheelchair child in the school, but the other children soon got used to it and treated her no differently from everybody else. It was deemed a privilege to be allowed to push her from one place to another (she still couldn't propel herself more than a yard or two) and there were always plenty of willing helpers. One day a boy was just pushing her backwards and forwards on the spot, and when the teacher intervened, thinking Claire needed defending, she looked up and said regally, 'I am being a lawnmower'!

Her imagination knew no bounds, and she learnt to read quickly and well which further fed her imagination. Her vocabulary was above average, so her stories were always interesting. The difficulty was that she had great trouble with writing. She knew what the letters were, but hadn't enough manual dexterity to get them on to paper so that they could be read. This problem was solved with the classroom computer. Claire easily learnt to use the keyboard, and although she couldn't type very quickly she was now able to write her stories down and do some excellent work. Her memory was good, and she enjoyed school as much as any of the children, within her limitations. Maths was her poorest subject.

As Claire progressed through the infant department her back became more of a nuisance to her. The bump had grown as she did, and was now large, tender and very vulnerable, as she often sat on the floor for various activities.

29

After the tragic fire at Bradford Football Club, new plastic surgery techniques had been developed for skin grafting, especially to the faces of the burn victims. A flat plastic balloon was inserted under a patch of good skin, and the balloon was gradually inflated until the skin stretched and grew. When the balloon was removed, there was then some 'spare' skin to cover the adjacent area. The patch stayed attached at one side so that it kept its blood supply, and because it was the patient's own skin there were no problems with rejection. The doctors now proposed to use this new technique on Claire's back, removing her bump and covering the area with her own skin.

The first step was to have a large balloon implanted under the skin between her shoulder blades, extending down nearly to waist level. Elvin took time off work again, and this time I stayed at the hospital as it was further away than our usual one. Claire was totally unbothered by being in hospital. We shared a room so that I could be with her all the time, and she took a great interest in everything that was going on. The only thing that upset her was missing lunch on the day of her operation, but the nurses promised to save her some chips. One of them privately confided to me that, although she would save them as promised, Claire wouldn't feel up to eating after the anaesthetic. She obviously didn't know Claire; while the others were sipping water and looking green, Claire ate her chips with gusto, and suffered no ill effects! She had to lie flat on her tummy for three days, but still managed to paint and play as they pushed her bed into the playroom. Then she was allowed up and they started to inflate the balloon. It had a long neck which ran to an injection port under the skin, and they had thoughtfully placed this where she couldn't feel, so that the filling of the balloon didn't distress her at all. We had two sessions of running salt water into it, and then we were allowed home.

Claire was perfectly well, but as the balloon was filled a little more each week it got very heavy and restricted her movements even further. It tired her to sit up for long periods, so she ended up going to school for mornings only. It also made her more difficult to handle as there were now two bumps to contend with, and none of her clothes would fit over the balloon. She had to wear her coat and cardigans back to front, and she didn't fit into her moulded seat at all well. She put up with it all with a good grace, however, and at last there was considered to be enough new skin to go ahead with the main operation to remove her spina bifida bump.

Elvin held the fort again and Claire and I took up residence in our usual hospital. Although it was within commuting distance this was to be such a major undertaking that I didn't want to leave her, and she was now old enough to worry. If everything was explained to her she was fine, but sometimes the doctors and nurses didn't have the time, and then her imagination took over and she feared the worst. It didn't help that everything took place on her back where she couldn't see what was going on, so I had to give her a running commentary to keep her happy.

The operation was very long but went well, and we then had a tedious spell of two weeks in bed, with Claire flat on her tummy, while everything healed up. At least, those two weeks were tedious for me, but Claire had so many visitors, cards, new toys and constant entertainment that she quite enjoyed herself. Maggi made her a brilliant 'no bumps' card, depicting a camel with its humps crossed out, and it was wonderful to see the sheet lying flat across Claire's back for the first time in six years. She was allowed up for the first time after tea on Bonfire Night, and the nurses found us a picture window, then turned all the lights off so that Claire could enjoy seeing the fireworks.

Although the most difficult part of the operation – the removal of the spina bifida bump – had gone perfectly to plan the amount of skin available to cover it hadn't been quite enough. The skin died at the far end of the graft because it was stretched too far, so a third operation was necessary to do a little patchwork.

We were allowed home for a week in between, and Claire revelled in sitting on the settee, lying painlessly on the floor, and her freedom from all bumps. She wasn't allowed to get her back wet, so we laid her along the ironing board with her head over the bath to wash her hair, which was now long enough to plait. It was rather precarious, and the situation not at all improved by everybody concerned getting a fit of the giggles, but at least she entered hospital for the third operation in a respectable condition. This hospital was the farthest away of them all, and by now Elvin had used up all his holiday allowances, but his firm allowed him to take time off without pay so that I could accompany Claire again.

The plastic surgery and burns units were full of post-Bonfire Night casualties (it put me off fireworks for life) so we were accommodated in the orthopaedic ward. Most of the children had their legs strung up on wires and were in for a long time, so there was a very relaxed atmosphere with plenty of visitors to provide interesting diversions. Christmas festivities start early in hospitals; they were making decorations already, and Claire was very thrilled when some ladies came with ingredients for Christmas puddings, and all the children were presented with real silver threepenny pieces.

As this latest operation was on the lower part of her back she couldn't feel it at all (she had no movement or feeling from the waist down) so the dressings and stitches didn't bother her one bit. Although she had the usual stint of being confined to lying on her tummy she was able to prop herself up on her elbows and so do a wide range of activities.

Once it was all over and we were home, the advantages of having a smooth back far outweighed any inconvenience over the last twelve weeks. Claire learnt to roll over on the floor, and eventually to get from lying to a sitting position without help. She could now sit on anything, and no longer needed a moulded seat so she was given a proper little child-sized wheelchair which would fold up to go into the car, which left more room for other people's pushchairs and bulk shopping The new wheelchair was also considerably easier to push. The old wheelchair frame with the moulded seat was very low, had no proper handles and wouldn't go up kerbs, so now life was easier in all sorts of ways.

The head teacher at Claire's school had a friend, head of another school, with several disabled children in her care. Some of these had electric wheelchairs designed especially for children, and I was invited to visit her school to see them in action. The plan was for Claire to have one if I thought it was suitable. I had never heard of them, but our head teacher was very impressed and took time out of her busy day to drive me to her friend's school on the other side of the county.

The chair had been invented by an engineer whose own daughter was disabled, for her use. Friends had seen it in action and asked him to make others for their children, and eventually he had set up a company to manufacture them. It was called a Turbo, and I was more than impressed when I saw one. It had a soft furry sheepskin seat, BMX wheels, and looked like a fun vehicle with its bright colour and chunky design. The battery and 'works' were housed in the boot, which had a flat carrying platform, and the whole thing was easily driven by a simple joystick. Its best feature was its ability to go up and down. The driver could go up high enough to sit at standard table height, right down so that they were sitting on the floor, or anywhere in between. This made it ideal for primary schools where tables are low (Claire couldn't get her knees underneath now that she had her new wheelchair) and for sitting at normal sized tables at home.

On the way home we decided that Claire would benefit from having a Turbo, and the head suggested that the school would attempt to raise the money for it. Such sophisticated chairs cost thousands of pounds, and are not available on the NHS. The next parent-teacher association meeting was informed of this, and willingly set up a fund-raising committee which swung into action immediately. Claire wrote a letter in her own words explaining what was happening, and all the children took a copy home. Here is what she put:

> Dear Mummies and Daddies,
>
> I have got a video of a new chair and I am writing to tell you about it. I go about in a wheelchair because I have got floppy legs. I struggle. My Mummy has seen a new Turbo chair. It goes up and down. A joystick operates it. Then I could answer the telephone and I could go down when I have finished on the telephone.
> I could reach the shelves at school and I could fit my knees under the table properly. I could get bricks off the floor and build them up high. When we have dancing I could push the joystick and go about.
> It would spend quite a lot of money though. Will you help us find some money? I would like a Turbo chair.
>
> With love from Claire.

We contacted the Turbo people and they arranged for a demonstration model to be brought to school for an afternoon. The local paper sent a reporter and photographer, and Claire met a Turbo for the first time. She drove it without any difficulty from the word go, and the whole school lined the playground to watch her put it through its paces. She twirled and circled very happily, went up and down numerous times, and had her photo taken for the local paper. The only sad moment was when she had to give it back – she had had a taste of freedom and wanted more!

All this publicity did wonders for the fund-raising, and we were able to place a firm order in a very short time. Claire chose a yellow Turbo, which was no surprise as it had long been her favourite colour. While we had the demo model at the school we had tried putting it in our car – it drove itself up ramps like a pair of skis – and found that although it went in the back of our estate it was too long for the tailgate to shut down. We would have to change our car again!

The school held various small fund-raising efforts, many of them organised by the children themselves, and three large events were due to take place. The first was a video disco, to be held in the evening, for adults; the second a strawberry tea during school time, for children and parents; and lastly a sponsored bounce, again during school time, when every child in the school would have exactly one minute on a bouncy castle, and collect sponsor money at so much per bounce.

In addition we received donations from many individuals and local organisations, and the fund grew very satisfactorily. Then, between the first two main events, the head teacher asked me to call in. Two local businessmen were in the habit of making a substantial donation once a year out of their profits, to help a child in the area, and had sent the school a cheque to cover the whole cost of the Turbo. We were now in the happy but rather embarrassing position of having too much money! Plans for the strawberry tea and sponsored bounce were well under way, so it was decided to carry on and hold them, but not to have any other fund-raising activities.

The delivery date for the Turbo – soon christened the Yellow Peril – was brought forward, and when Claire's class went to the farm to pick the strawberries for the tea she was able to drive herself through the fields and go down to ground level to help with the picking.

The weather was kind for both the strawberry tea and the bouncy castle (which turned out to be a bouncy dragon!) and the fund swelled even more. Some children made great leaping bounces which took two or three seconds each so they didn't fit

35

many into their minute, but Claire, who could only sit on her bottom and bob up and down on the spot, managed eighty-seven and was very proud of herself.

The whole school, reinforced by many adults, assembled around the playground again for the formal presentation of the Turbo by the chairman of the fund-raising committee. He was an ambulanceman and well used to lifting people, but he later admitted to real nervousness as he lifted Claire out of her wheelchair and into the Turbo with a couple of hundred people watching him! He and his wife had included a couple of nice touches, like a helium balloon tied to the back and a cuddly toy sitting on the carrying platform, and Claire did a lap of honour around the playground with the biggest grin imaginable on her face.

She wrote a thank you letter which all the children took home the following day:

To everybody who helped me get my Turbo.

Thank you very much. It is very comfy and furry. I have only had it a few days and this is what I can do.
I can pick things up when I drop them.
I went across the grass to see a mother duck and six ducklings.
When my baby throws her rattle out I can get it for her.
I can put bottles out on the step for the milkman.
I brought a box of shopping home for Mummy. I can follow her round the house now.
Every day I am finding out more things that I can do. I love having my Turbo.
Thank you all very much.

With love from Claire xxx.

It was decided to use some of the extra money in the fund to buy Claire her own computer, so that she could always have access to one and not have to take turns with the rest of the class. The rest was left as a maintenance fund for future use as other needs arose, and for servicing the Turbo and such expenses as replacement batteries.

The Turbo made a great difference to Claire, enabling her to take part in almost all activities at school. It had a standing frame which could be used instead of the seat, and Claire's hospital frame fitted inside it so that now she could be mobile whilst standing up. This was a great thrill for her; she rushed around the playground in a vertical position and could reach the top bookshelves when necessary as she could still go up and down. She made discoveries such as the kitchen floor being cold, and learnt to drive expertly. The Turbo was also very useful for such activities as stripping wallpaper, painting walls, picking apples and helping to decorate the Christmas tree! Her reversing was very much envied by Liz, who failed her driving test the first time due to poor reversing.

The Yellow Peril became such a part of Claire's life that it was regarded as almost an extension of her body. One of her teachers described her as 'a normal little girl who happens to have a metal lower half'. She joined the Brownies and was put in the Imps, which seemed entirely appropriate, and led a very full and happy life.

One of the major events in her calendar was being a bridesmaid. Her school helper was to be married in the summer holidays, and early in the year she invited Claire to be one of her five bridesmaids. This was the focus of attention for the next six months, with Claire enjoying every aspect of the planning, dressmaking, fittings and general preparations. On the day of the wedding she was bursting with importance – anybody would have thought she was responsible for the whole ceremony! Everybody had posies of flowers, and the Turbo had its own little matching flower arrangement on the boot so that she even looked beautiful from the rear when driving up the aisle.

Claire happened to be directly in front of the bride and groom when the confetti throwing started, and was so liberally showered with it that I was hoovering bits out of the fur on her seat for days. A liberal dose also went down the ventilation holes and into the works, but Turbos are made of stern stuff and it didn't suffer any ill effects.

I had our car parked close to the church, ready to take Claire to the reception, but she very firmly informed me that she was going in the white Rolls with the other bridesmaids. I was permitted to follow humbly behind with the Turbo while she travelled in style and waved regally to the guests!

On the very rare occasions that the Yellow Peril was 'off the road' for service or repair, and Claire was back in her push wheelchair, she was a different child. She immediately became a spectator rather than joining in, which showed how much her Turbo had transformed her life.

5

Penny

At Christmas time, just after Claire's fifth birthday, we were asked if we would take another handicapped new baby. This little girl's mother was mentally inadequate, and nobody knew who the father was; I gathered it was thought to be another patient at the day centre she attended. Under these circumstances the baby hadn't got much going for her.

Although our hearts went out to this unwanted scrap as soon as we heard about her, we had to refuse as we already had Thomas, a five week old baby boy, and I just couldn't manage another baby as well as the other children. Elvin was at work all day, and we were both heavily involved at the church. We didn't have a minister; different men took the leadership and Elvin was currently doing it, as well as his tape recordings. I still had my Sunday School class, and was also church secretary. Aunty Shirley was no longer on the scene, and I now had deadlines morning and afternoon getting Claire to and from school. I have never quite understood why a disabled child is taken by taxi from home to its special school each day, but if the same child attends an ordinary school (in our case much nearer to home) the transportation is up to the parents.

In addition, Thomas was one of those babies who cries all the time for no apparent reason. He seemed to want to do more than he was capable of, and he was really hard work. All the time though I kept thinking about little Penny, and wondering how she was getting on – I knew the social workers were having difficulties in finding foster parents for her, so she was still in hospital. She wasn't thriving, and eventually it was discovered that she needed an operation. Before a baby is born it doesn't use its lungs so a little blood vessel bypasses them. At birth this bypass closes off so that blood then flows through the lungs and the baby starts to breathe. Penny's hadn't closed properly, so they had to operate as she was getting quite blue. By the time she'd had her stitches out and was able to leave hospital, Thomas had moved to his adoptive family and we were able to take Penny. She was then six weeks old, and was our fifty-third child.

Like all children, Claire never tired of hearing stories about herself, how we had all gone to the hospital to see her, and all that happened afterwards. She was now delighted to be part of the inspection committee, as it was on the familiar ground of 'her' hospital, although we hadn't been to the heart ward before.

Penny was a really pathetic sight. She was very small and thin, very pale, and didn't react to much. When she cried she opened her mouth but was too weak to make any sound, little tears just rolled down her cheeks. She had an oddly shaped head with her ears set very low down – my first comment on seeing her was that I hoped she'd never need glasses, as there was nothing to hook them on to! Her eyes were blue and she had quite a mop of hair so blonde as to be almost silver. She was festooned with several wires leading to different monitors, but nobody had any questions other than how soon we could take her home with us.

Penny turned out to be quite a challenge. I had gained a reputation of being 'good with babies', but this one taxed my skills to the limit. For most of her short life Penny had been tube fed as she was too weak to suck; the hospital had introduced her to bottles before she came to us, but she was still very weak. She tired herself out before she had taken nearly enough, and was painfully slow. Despite cutting the top off the teat with the nail scissors, and making a hole you could drive a bus through, she took two hours to drink two ounces of milk.

As she was on four-hourly feeds round the clock, twelve hours out of each twenty-four were spent just feeding her. The rest of the family had to be fed too, clean clothes made available, and a minimum of sleep fitted in, which left absolutely no time for anything else. The house rapidly slid downhill and I was powerless to do anything about it.

Then one Monday morning I answered the door to find a lady from church on the doorstep. I knew her by sight but not well, as she lived in the next village and we never met except at church. She swept past me saying, 'You've got your hands full with that baby. I've come to help.' She headed for the kitchen, more chaotic than ever after the ravages of the weekend, and restored it to cleanliness and order before the morning was over.

Not content with this charitable act, she came morning after morning until the whole house shone, and made herself indispensable. After a while I insisted that she receive some pay for all her work, so 'Aunty Do' became a permanent fixture, taking over where Aunty Shirley had left off.

As Penny grew older, she became a little easier to manage. She was stronger, and could now cry like a kitten – not loudly, but infinitely preferable to her former silent anguish. She never learnt to take a bottle properly, but once she progressed to mush on a spoon she put on weight and looked much better. She had a decidedly sweet tooth, refusing dinners unless really hungry, and accepting puddings very readily. We sometimes resorted to alternating spoonfuls of savoury and sweet, but she soon developed the ability to spit out the scrambled eggs, or whatever, while swallowing the strawberry yoghurt!

Penny remained very developmentally delayed, but she smiled and chuckled and recognised 'her' people. She included Aunty Do amongst these, and the feeling was mutual. Aunty Do had brought up five boys of her own, and handled Penny with loving patience which was rewarded by some very special moments. Penny didn't have milestones, but inchstones, and Aunty Do was as thrilled as we were by every tiny little bit of progress. Claire and Penny got on very well together, Maggi and Liz loved them both, and we were the only parents either of them had ever known, so we applied to Social Services to adopt them. Foster parents have no rights – if a decision is made to place a child with somebody else, there is nothing we can do about it. We couldn't have borne for Claire or Penny to leave us; they were now part of the family.

The formalities took some time, not helped by the postal strike which delayed many of the papers, but we eventually went to court on a bright October day when Claire was nearly seven and Penny nearly two (they both have December birthdays).

Claire had a great sense of occasion; she loved pomp and ceremony and special events, so she was very disappointed when the judge was just a man in a dark suit, looking like any other businessman. Apparently he dressed informally so as not to intimidate the children, but Claire, who was never shy, asked him to please put his robes and wig on, so that he looked like a judge! He was very nice about it, and held up the proceedings while he robed, then willingly posed for photographs with us afterwards.

Claire had no middle name when she came to us, so upon her adoption she gained the middle name 'Ruth' after the biblical Ruth who said, 'Where you go, I will go; where you live, I will live; your people shall be my people, and your God my God', which seems to me to capture the essence of becoming one family. Liz prepared a sumptuous buffet on the Sunday, and after a special service of welcome and dedication, a houseful of friends celebrated the addition to their midst of Penny Michelle Rose and Claire Ruth Rose. We asked Aunty Do to be Penny's godmother, and her sister, Aunty Margaret, to be Claire's, and they both accepted joyfully.

Penny entered the nursery class of our nearest special school, and continued to make slow progress. She looked so tiny to be whisked away in the minibus every morning, but she didn't seem to mind. I had my hands full getting Claire ready for school, so Aunty Do came at 7.30am each day to see to Penny. She was one of the very few people who could feed her successfully, and managed to get a man-sized bowl of very sweet Ready Brek into her every morning before the minibus came.

It was Aunty Do who coaxed Penny to take her own weight, and eventually to stand for a moment unaided, by the time she was about three. By now Maggi and Liz had gone through O' levels, A' levels, driving tests and clearing houses and had left home. We were still having other foster children, but not as intensely as before. One toddler came to us while his foster parents were away for a week's holiday. He came out in chicken pox during his stay and then three weeks later, while we were away at the seaside, Penny and one of the older boys who was then with us came out in spots. It wasn't much of a nuisance; we just avoided public places and kept sand off their spots. Claire appointed herself head nurse and dabbed on calamine lotion as necessary, and we thought nothing of it.

But after we had been home for a few weeks Penny started to lose weight, and developed a bad chest. She had pneumonia, which is apparently a rare complication of chicken pox. Then she began to swell around her tummy, while still losing weight on her arms and legs. Hospital tests showed heart failure, and she was given a whole array of medication after a week in hospital to stabilise her.

That spell in hospital was very difficult. I couldn't stay with her because I was the only one who could care for Claire's needs, so Elvin and I worked a shuttle service. He went at the crack of dawn to get Penny up and fed, and I took over as soon as Claire was at school. I had to leave in time to collect Claire again, and Elvin went again at teatime and stayed to put Penny to bed. Luckily we had a second car by now, but we also had a two month old Down's baby who required four-hourly feeds, as well as two boys and a girl about Claire's age.

Penny was allowed home and the pressure eased, but she wasn't her former happy self. Getting the medicine into her was a struggle, to put it mildly, and she gradually lost ground. In the middle of October she was admitted to hospital again to see if more drugs would help, but she didn't respond. We were told that a heart transplant would be the only answer but handicapped children weren't offered these – there weren't enough to go round the normal children, even if we had agreed.

The disruption to the family was so great and the shuttle service so wearing that we asked if we could bring Penny home. The doctors had explained that it was just a matter of time until her heart failed completely, but they had no idea whether it would be days, weeks or months away. Being in hospital was doing her no good, so they let us take her home.

We explained to the other children that Penny had a bad heart, and it couldn't go on for much longer, but it was quite difficult for them to understand. They had the vague idea that only old people died; everybody else had medicine or an operation and got better, although it was quite obvious to them that Penny was ill. Her tummy was tightly swollen, but her arms, legs and face were skeletally thin, like children in the most harrowing Oxfam posters.

Penny just wanted to be held. Aunty Do stayed hours longer than she should have done, nursing her, and the older four children went to school as usual. Our Down's baby went back home the next Friday, which was the day before Penny and Claire's second adoptive birthday. Because Penny's real birthday was only three days before Christmas, we had taken to celebrating adoption day instead, with a cake and candles as if it was her birthday, and ignoring the Christmas date.

Because Penny was so poorly we just had a family tea (although with seven of us every meal was something of a party!) and they all blew out her two candles for her. I didn't take her to church the next day and sometime during Sunday night her heart stopped beating, in her sleep. The first I knew was that I woke up to silence; usually Penny whimpered at about 6.30am to let me know she was awake. Now it was 7.30 and I had awoken naturally for the first time in ages. I went in to her, and she wasn't breathing. When I touched her cheek it was cold, and when the doctor came he said she had probably died in the very early hours of the morning.

I had very mixed feelings about her death. It had been so hard to watch her suffering that I had been praying that she would die sooner rather than later, and part of me was relieved that it was over. The other part was missing her dreadfully; I burst into tears all over the doctor, and said, 'I'm happy really!'

Telling the other children was very hard. I went in to Claire and said, 'Penny went to heaven in the night', and we had a little weep together. When the others came down Claire wanted to tell them, and I 'phoned Liz. Maggi had been staying for a few days, and she was able to register Penny's death for us before she went home.

Elvin organised the undertaker, and Claire stayed at home as she was so upset. The other three went to school, and Claire went too next day. Suddenly I had nothing to do! From having two babies to feed, bathe, or nurse literally every second of the day, I now had none. I just didn't know what to do with my hands, so I started to knit. Everybody had at least one jumper or cardigan before Christmas. Social Services offered to take the three foster children elsewhere for a spell, but that would have only made matters worse.

Penny's funeral was a joyful occasion. We had all her favourite choruses, jumpy ones that she loved to clap to – she couldn't sing or talk but she liked music, and would stand between my knees and clap. We had no doubt but that she was now perfectly well and whole in heaven with all her handicaps left behind. She had always loved anything bright and sparkly, and I thought how much she would now be enjoying the lights of heaven. I had read somewhere that an unborn baby can see light dimly if bright sunlight shines on the mother's tummy, but it must bear no relation to colours and rainbows and all the delightful things we see after birth. I thought that going to heaven must be very similar; what we see on earth is a very dim preparation for what is to come. It was very comforting to think how Penny would now be revelling in all this glory, and in her new and perfect form.

There is a graveyard in our village, and we had Penny buried there. Although it meant starting a new row, the rector kindly arranged for her grave to be next to the path so that Claire could reach it easily.

I talked a lot with Claire about how only Penny's body had died; her soul was alive and well. I compared it to a butterfly coming out of a chrysalis. Penny was now soaring free, and all that was left was her old shell. Claire was not quite nine at the time, and was well able to understand this concept. Maggi and Liz came home for Penny's funeral, and were very much distressed by the sight of her tiny coffin, but Claire was so convinced by my explanation that I don't think she thought there was anything much in it at all, and went through the service and burial quite calmly.

For the next few months, however, Claire couldn't go to sleep unless I sat with her. We continued to talk often about what heaven was like, and how Penny would be running about and enjoying herself, but we all missed her. Claire felt so sorry for Aunty Do, bereft of her god-daughter, that she invited her to become her godmother now, as well as Aunty Margaret. She thought of this entirely independently, and Aunty Do was touched.

Very gradually, Claire would go to sleep alone, but only if everyone else was safely upstairs in bed. I think she had a fear, never put into words, that somebody else might die next. She couldn't relax enough to sleep unless we were all accounted for. She thought we had gone to bed, but actually we had a video upstairs, and watched films with headphones on so that she wouldn't hear the noise!

6

A full-time job

As the years passed, fostering became such a way of life for us that we couldn't imagine not doing it. There was no doubt that it was hard work, and it curtailed our social life considerably, but we felt that we were doing a worthwhile job which was very satisfying. At the same time Elvin was getting increasingly dissatisfied with his job; watching numbers on a VDU screen in a basement office seemed so pointless when there was so much to be done with the children. Many of them didn't have a father figure at home and they appreciated having him around. Eventually we decided to apply to Barnardo's to see if we could have several of their children living in our home, and both of us be the full-time care workers for them.

When we talked to our social worker about this, she said there was no need to approach Barnardo's – we could do the same thing for our existing Social Services department, without the need for any extra approval. There was no shortage of children, and we could start any time we liked. So Elvin gave in his notice, we bought the little second-hand car so that we could be in two places at once (I was tied to Claire's school time-table in term time, which was fairly restricting) and we became full-time foster parents.

Our first recruit in this new venture was our fifty-fourth child, a ten year old who stayed until he was nearly thirteen. He'd had an unsettled childhood of moves between one parent and the other, with spells in different foster homes, and came to us from a children's home. Gaps in his schooling meant that he couldn't even say the months of the year in order, but Claire soon taught him those. There was nothing wrong with his intelligence, he'd just had too many moves to absorb much. He took the view of authority that it was all right as long as you didn't get caught, and he also had a rather vague separation of fact and fiction. These combined into one curious episode that was rather wearing at the time.

Our local telephone exchange was being refurbished, and the outmoded equipment was stacked behind the building awaiting removal. Of course the local lads discovered these interesting items, which included terminals and electrical components, and ferreted about amongst them. On the way to school next day our lad was flashing a five pound note (lifted from Elvin, we later discovered). When a friend asked him where he'd got it, he spun a yarn about selling car radios he and his cousin had stolen, and this fiver was his share of the profits. He told the friend that all the car radios were stacked behind the telephone exchange, and offered to show him after school. The friend obviously believed him, and also had a conscience, so he told his teacher when he got to school. It was a different school from the one our lad was attending, but his head rang the other head and told her, and was immediately advised to ring the police. Of course the police took it seriously, and the first we knew about any of this was when a constable rang our doorbell in pursuit of his enquiries! Eventually it was all straightened out and found to be untrue, but it didn't do much for his reputation in the village.

This lad had a lot going for him – he was friendly and had a tender side which could be reached quite easily. He could feel for other people, especially those depicted on the TV as being in need, and worked quite hard at various relief efforts organised by school and church. He was considerate and companionable with Claire, but found it impossible to maintain friendships with other boys of his own age. He started trying to buy their friendship, which led us into a masterpiece of detective work.

One of our neighbours had a severely disabled daughter, and after our lad had been in to play with her three year old son, she discovered that the daughter's attendance allowance was missing. It was £80 in £20 notes which she had collected at the post office that day, and thought she'd left it in her handbag in the hall. She came across to see if he knew anything about it, not to accuse him, but because she was worried. He convincingly denied all knowledge of it, and when he went out to play again I hunted round his room, but there was no sign of it. This was a distinct relief, as at other times I'd found other people's watches under his mattress, and I didn't like to think that he was now helping himself to large sums of money.

The next day our neighbour put up a notice in the post office, thinking she might have dropped the money on the way home, but there was no response. Elvin went the rounds of the local paper shops, and discovered that another boy had been in with a £20 note, buying loads of sweets, with no reasonable explanation when the shopkeeper asked where he'd got the money. I knew this boy sometimes played with ours, so when I got home I 'phoned the parents of all the boys I could think of who played with him. After considerable sifting and questioning, we discovered that three of his friends had recently been given £20 notes by him. The three sets of parents were horrified, and made the boys come round to me to repay the money. Anything they had spent was to be repaid out of their pocket money and they were all suitably chastened.

We laid this evidence before our lad when he came home, and he then admitted that he had taken the money. He seemed to think that giving most of it away was a mitigating circumstance! He had spent £7 on sweets, which he had mostly distributed at school, and had the remaining £13 in his pocket. He was marched across to the neighbour's house, where he returned the money and agreed to pay the missing £7 at a pound a week out of his pocket money. The neighbour did not want to involve the police, but we decided to have a talk with them in the hope that it would be a deterrent for the future. Elvin accompanied him to the police station, where he was lectured by a sergeant and given a warning. When they returned he breezed into the kitchen and said, 'Aunty Jenny, can I have a piece of fruit?' So much for being subdued!

A year or more later he helped himself to £22 from a teacher's handbag and was suspended, and eventually he left us under unpleasant circumstances. He had been excluded from school for over six weeks and no other local school would take him, so that having him hanging about the house all the time became intolerable.

All this time there were other children coming and going, ranging from five weeks to sixteen years old. Most of them weren't so wearing as the first lad, possibly because they stayed for a shorter time. We had two little sisters of one and a half and three and a half who fought like cat and dog Whatever the little one had the bigger one wanted, even if it had lain untouched all day until then. This might sound quite usual, but she took it to extremes. She even got upset if her sister spat her toothpaste out first when they were cleaning their teeth! Eventually a decision was made to separate them, and they were adopted by two different families. Both ended up as the youngest girl, each with an older brother, and they have done very well.

Another happy ending came for a little girl of seven, who had been severely neglected. She had more or less lived on the streets after school, as her mother stayed out late, and had been fed by neighbours taking pity on her. She was adopted by a childless couple and so gained an American granny; when they went to the States to visit her they had a trip to Disneyland. It must have been all a neglected waif could have dreamt of, and our Claire was green with envy!

Claire became part of the care team with these children. It was amazing how many of them didn't really know how to play, but Claire gently took them in hand. The dressing up box was very popular, especially with the older girls. Sometimes whole days were spent devising elaborate plays, acted for a captive audience of two who often hadn't a clue as to what the plot was all about. However, the actors obviously enjoyed themselves, so the applause was always enthusiastic.

Claire seemed to have that rare quality called empathy, of knowing how another person is feeling. Sometimes this wasn't always a good thing – when she was in the infants she would always join in if another child cried. As she got older it enabled her to get on well with all the children we had, and to quickly become their friend. It was interesting that Maggi and Liz had acted as agony aunts for their friends at school, and later at college, and Claire seemed to be following in their footsteps. As she moved through the school into the upper juniors she became the class peacemaker, negotiating for the various parties in playground squabbles and becoming the confidante of many of her class. She was totally devoid of self-pity, and developed a strong social conscience. If there were any appeals for aid on programmes like *Blue Peter* or *Newsround*, or at school, Claire was always eager to help, and organised the whole family into sending off old keys, packets of rice, or whatever else was required. She also became involved in the welfare of whales, dolphins and African elephants, supervising the shopping to make sure our tuna was dolphin-friendly and our aerosols CFC free. We were also all gently bullied into saving every possible waste item for recycling.

Claire developed a passion for hospital programmes. Elvin, who was squeamish, had to look the other way sometimes during *Jimmy's*, about St. James Hospital in Leeds, but Claire lapped it all up and couldn't get enough. A lot of information was given about organ transplants, and one day she turned to me and informed me that she wanted her 'bits' used when she no longer needed them. She also approved of me carrying a donor card, and couldn't understand why everybody didn't.

Most of the children we took now were expected to need more time spent with them, because of their unsettled lives due to family difficulties. Of the next thirty-two children we looked after, only two were living in a stable family unit with both parents. Of these two, one was disabled and came while her mother had an operation, and the other came for one weekend a month to give his mum a break as she was finding her large unruly family too much for her.

All the rest lived with one parent, and very often it was the tensions between that parent and the other one that had caused the disruption. For other children the problem was the inability of the sole parent to care adequately for them. There were many different reasons for this – none of them deliberate – but the result was always a neglected child, either physically or emotionally, or both.

These children always found it hard, even impossible, to form lasting and deep relationships with new adults. One little girl came to us three separate times. She had been placed with different prospective adoptive parents, but each time it had all broken down catastrophically because she was unable to maintain a family bond. Two others came twice, and we were delighted when one of them was successfully and happily adopted. Only a handful of children returned home to stable and improved lives, and yet their loyalty to their parents was very strong. We always had to be very careful not to appear critical when speaking of their families as the children were very sensitive in this area, and defended their parents to the hilt. Many felt responsible for them, and worried about their well-being as if they were the adult instead of the child. The loyalty shown by these children was so deep and strong that they could see no fault in their parent. This meant that they couldn't believe the reason for being taken away, and so they were very resentful of social workers, and by implication foster parents. They saw being 'in care' as a terrible fate, themselves as social outcasts, and felt that they carried a stigma which was going to blight their lives forever.

We had one girl, scarcely into her teens, who caused us a lot of heartache. The original 'phone call described her as 'thirteen going on twenty-five', and she was so streetwise that moving to our quiet village caused her considerable culture shock. She'd been used to fending for herself, coming and going as she pleased, and couldn't adapt to an organised life. We made it clear that we expected her to come home from school, and that if she was delayed she should 'phone. There was a public 'phone in the school foyer, we gave her change and our 'phone number in her pencil case, but still she regularly left home after breakfast to go to school, and didn't return until about 11pm, with no 'phone call or message.

She was very evasive about where she'd been, and often gave false information about being invited to tea with various friends. When I 'phoned the parents to check they knew nothing about it. One day an expensive pair of American jeans turned up in the washing basket. I had to turn detective again and found that they belonged to a friend's mother, who was wondering where her best jeans had got to!

I discovered that many of her evenings were spent at a lad's house. He was older than she, and they were alone in the house as his mother was a barmaid who worked late hours. She went there straight from school and stayed until just before his mother came home, and then had to make her way back home along three miles of dark country roads. By then the buses had stopped running, so she either walked or borrowed the boy's bike (without lights, and much too big for her). She'd sometimes arrive home soaking wet, having kept us up and ever more worried for her safety, and would give no explanations.

The last straw came when she stayed out all night. When she wasn't home by midnight I 'phoned some of her friends, having to apologise for waking them up, and found out that she had told them she was going to spend the night in the local park. This area was known to be the haunt of all the local undesirables, glue sniffers and worse, so we called the police. They came at 2am and woke the whole house, very much upsetting Claire. She had already gone through agonies every time the girl was missing at tea-time, and I had great difficulty in getting her to settle at night when one of the family was unaccounted for – this was all happening in the period following Penny's death. Recently a beloved great aunt had died, closely followed by the death of Elvin's mum, so it was all brought back to her. Both ladies were in their eighties, and we talked often about how they would be having a marvellous tea party (both were Welsh and great talkers) and how Penny would be enjoying their company in heaven, but Claire was again finding it difficult to sleep because not all the members of the family were safe.

The police didn't find the girl until the following afternoon; she'd been at a friend's house all the time. She'd told the mother that she had permission to stay the night, and nobody seemed to find it odd that she hadn't even a toothbrush with her. We asked the Social Services to accommodate her somewhere else, as the strain was too great. Her social worker told me that once she was over our doorstep we were no longer responsible for her, but I found it impossible to switch off. By mutual agreement we were not asked to take any more teenagers, although others we'd had before had been perfectly happy.

About this time the law about children in care was changed; fostering was to be used a lot less. If at all possible the family would be kept together by putting in home helps and any other means available to take the strain off and leave the children with their parents. If this wasn't possible, the children would stay with a relative, godparent or even a neighbour, so that they were in familiar surroundings. Failing that they would be placed with a nearby foster family so that the natural family could visit daily. All this must have been good for the children, but it did us out of a job! We were a long way out of town, so obviously nearer foster parents were used first, and also children were now brought into care in only the most difficult situations. Since this often involved teenagers, whom we no longer took, the future looked a bit empty.

During Claire's last year in primary school we only had one extra member of the family, an eleven year old girl called Ann, who had learning difficulties. We had now cared for eighty-six children, thirty-six of them during the three and a half years since Elvin had given up his job, so it felt very quiet.

Claire and Ann were both at school all day, so we did the decorating and got the garden straight – years of footballers hadn't improved it much – and dug a pond because Claire wanted frogs. I'd fancied having a pond for years but having toddlers about had always prevented it.

My mother died in the spring, and my sister invited us to visit her out in South Africa. As we had been left some money we decided to go, it was now or never because once Claire started high school she wouldn't be able to take the extra time off, and it wasn't worth going for less than a month. Maggi moved into our house to look after Ann. She could still go to work while Ann was at school as she would be able to use our car. October half-term week was included in our holiday, so Maggi booked that week off and planned all sorts of outings. With a car at her disposal and no restrictions of having to consider wheelchair access for Claire, the two of them were looking forward to a great week of excursions.

Claire and I had never flown before, and Elvin only one short hop, so the journey was an exciting part of the holiday. The airline took both the Turbo and Claire's push wheelchair at no extra charge, which we thought was very good of them. My sister had sent a long shopping list of things she couldn't buy in South Africa, from Clarks sandals to paper cake cases, and we also took Christmas presents. Luckily we weren't going to need much in the way of clothes, T-shirts and sunglasses being the order of the day. One case was filled with Claire's toilet requirements alone, but we just managed to keep within the weight allowance.

Our journey was long but uneventful. A nurse accompanied us on to and off each plane, another member of the airport staff whisked us through all the formalities when we changed at Johannesburg, and it was all very painless. It was an overnight flight, and Claire slept better than either of us, arriving in Cape Town as fresh as a daisy and bursting with excitement. The family met us at the airport with two cars. We put the Turbo (in pieces) in one boot and our cases in the other, then headed home for a very necessary cup of tea.

October is springtime in South Africa, and the climate was like a good summer in England, warm and breezy, and everywhere covered in flowers. The seeds we grow so carefully in our gardens are wild flowers, even weeds, there! It was quite cold at night, which we weren't expecting. One of our first purchases was a hot water bottle for Claire, not an easy thing to find in South Africa.

The weather soon got quite hot, and Claire needed a sun hat. Her head was too big for a bought one, so she chose some bright red cotton material with white spots and I made her one. My sister promptly christened it 'the jam pot cover', and Claire wore it everywhere. She revelled in the freedom of being able to wear just a dress, socks and strappy sandals, as in England her legs were never warm even with long socks, two pairs of leg-warmers and long trousers, worn with clumpy hospital boots.

The month just flew by. It was our first holiday without anybody else's children for fourteen years, and a real treat. It was our silver wedding anniversary year, and my fiftieth birthday, and we really felt we were celebrating in style. Our brother-in-law owned a garage and was able to lend us a car, so we could go out and about where we pleased, although South Africa isn't very wheelchair-friendly. On one of our excursions we travelled down to Cape Point and on our way there discovered two whales. They were close to the shore along Chapman's Peak Drive at the bottom of a steep cliff, and Claire was ecstatic that she could see them clearly. She had long been interested in whales, but had never expected to see any in the flesh in their own environment.

Claire made a huge impression wherever we went. There didn't seem to be any other disabled children about, but she carried on just as she did in England, visiting shops and public places and chatting to everybody. She had recently moved from Brownies to Guides, and she went to both with her cousins. The Guides made her very welcome, and cheerfully included her in many of their indoor and outdoor pursuits. She also went to some school events, and generally gained a large extension to her fan club.

For the last year or so Claire and I had sometimes played a game in the car on the way to and from school. This involved throwing a story back and forth, each adding a bit and passing it back at a crucial point. It featured a dragon's adventures, and Claire's imagination had turned into an interesting story. Now that we were on holiday and had some time on our hands we polished it a bit and got it written down, giving it the title 'Dragongold'. The idea is that the main story is read aloud to younger children, then they are given a simplified version of it, with the same pictures, to read for themselves. Claire wanted two simplified versions, one very easy and one moderately so, which involved quite a lot of work. She had the idea, and I was expected to do the donkey work!

We returned home nicely tanned and loaded with gifts for her schoolfriends, to the shock of late November in England: bare trees, foggy nights and about a twenty-degree drop in temperature. Maggi, Liz and Ann were very pleased to see us – and their presents – and we soon settled back into the routine. Claire's eleventh birthday would soon be upon us, then it wasn't long to Christmas and the holiday in the sun had done us a world of good. For the first time in her life Claire got through the winter without repeated bouts of tonsillitis, and she also started to grow at an amazing rate.

In the next year we changed churches to a nearer one, and Elvin soon became very involved in various activities, including editing the recording of the Sunday services and distributing the tapes. Eventually he became responsible for the production of the monthly newsletter and he also used the computer to make an array of posters every week for the notice boards.

We still didn't have any more children, so the social worker linked us up with some families who needed respite care for their disabled children. They came to us for one or two days every month or so, to give their parents some time off. Ann was still with us, but we felt very underemployed, having been used to a houseful for so long.

7

Growing up

As Claire neared the end of her time at primary school, there were many changes in her life. She had grown so much that the Turbo no longer met her needs, so the physio at the hospital recommended a similar vehicle called a Skwirrel. The odd spelling was because it came from Holland, and had recently started to be imported into the UK. It did everything the Turbo did, but was bigger and could take an adult's weight. It also had lights for going out at night, which Claire did quite a lot now.

We couldn't ask the school to start fund-raising again, so the physio suggested we approach two national charities, Open Doors and The Royal Variety Club. Both agreed to help and Claire was responsible for selling twelve hundred gold hearts that February, with help from Maggi and Liz at their respective work places.

Claire got her Skwirrel at Easter, and we also bought a trailer to transport it in. Although it was just possible to get it into the car it was so heavy and bulky that it left no room for anybody besides Claire and me, so a trailer solved the problem neatly. It also caused some other problems – parking was much more difficult as we now needed a double space, and Claire's orange badge only covered us for one. Also I found it impossible to reverse with the trailer on, and her school was down a cul-de-sac. It meant unhooking to turn round, which was time consuming and awkward, but worth it as the Skwirrel was a great asset. It still went down to the floor, but also up much higher. Claire could now reach the top of our tall fridge, the washing line and high light switches, and could also be at eye level with her friends when they were standing up. It also had indicators which could both be switched on at once as hazard flashers, which she found very useful at discos!

Claire's helper at school had been with her for years and they were really good friends so it came as a great blow to Claire to discover that she wouldn't automatically transfer with her to the high school. The idea of leaving the security of her familiar primary school was causing a lot of worries: Claire didn't say much, but she started twiddling her hair so hard that she pulled it out and looked quite bald.

The high school had a policy of linking with its feeder primaries during the last two years before the children went there so Claire had paid a few visits already for various fun events and musical productions, notably *Joseph and the Amazing Technicolour Dreamcoat,* when we were ushered to stage-side seats and nearly choked by the over-enthusiastic smoke machine operators! During her last term the music teachers from the high school went into each primary school and taught the children the songs from *Noah*, then they all met together, reinforced by the existing first year pupils, and gave proper performances in the high school's drama studio. Claire enjoyed all this immensely, and as we went home after the last night she said, 'You know, I feel part of that school already.' She stopped pulling her hair out, and we were very much relieved.

At about the same time her helper became pregnant; we had to invent a fiction about a strained back as she didn't want to be lifting heavy weights, so I went in at lunch times to do the toileting. Just before the end of the term Claire was sworn to secrecy and told the great news. She was overjoyed and told her helper, 'You'll be a lovely mum as you've had so much practice looking after me!'

Lifting Claire was getting to be quite a problem. She was totally unable to take any weight on her floppy legs, and although she could roll out of her chair at ground level, she couldn't get back in without help. The council had extended our downstairs toilet to a proper bathroom, and had thoughtfully provided a changing surface on top of a row of cupboards where Claire could be dried and dressed at a comfortable working height. We had a bath hoist, but she still needed to be lifted in and out of bed, on and off the toilet, and in and out of the car. This last was solved with a car-top hoist, as the lift-and-twist movement wasn't doing my back any good, but for everything else I just gathered her into my arms and heaved. As she approached seven stones I was beginning to feel the strain, not so much in my back as in my arms, especially the elbows. I wasn't quite sure what we were going to do as she grew ever taller and heavier.

A friend of ours had a baby who was delightful, but very hard work. She once said, 'I don't mind, because I enjoy her so much', and this was exactly how I felt about Claire. As she grew older she was extremely good company, with a wicked sense of humour and an endless supply of games to play in the long periods we spent closeted in the bathroom together.

We have met many parents of disabled children who have been racked with guilt since the child was born. Even if the doctors have assured them that nothing they did (or didn't do) caused the disability, they have been unable to accept this. Others were angry that their child was less than perfect, which led to years of bitterness. Because Claire and Penny were adopted by us as known quantities we escaped both of these situations, and were able to enjoy them.

This doesn't mean I didn't have any worries about Claire's future. Every mother of teenage girls has anxieties which are part of the job, and there is a universal burden for parents of disabled children of 'What will happen to them when I'm gone?' One day I was driving home from taking Claire to school when a car coming the other way crashed into me, having just overtaken on a blind bend. Mercifully I was only shaken, although the car was severely damaged, but it could have been much worse. Nobody can guarantee good health at all times, and I sometimes worried about who would look after Claire if I was out of action for any reason. As a Christian I was able to hand these worries over to God to take care of, but they had a nasty habit of trying to resurface.

The one thing I have learnt, though, from half a century on this earth is that worry gets me nowhere. By the time the situation I have been worrying about arrives, there are usually so many unforeseen circumstances making the situation sufficiently different from what was expected that all the worrying was wasted anyway!

Practical problems were solved as we went along, although I did try to keep one step ahead so that I had already given some thought to possible solutions. Claire was inventive and willing to try anything once, and there were very few things she couldn't do even if it meant using unorthodox means. I could see that the time would soon come when she wanted to sit on her friends' beds and indulge in hours of girl talk, but this was going to be difficult as she couldn't even get into their houses, let alone up into their bedrooms. She'd had her share of boyfriends throughout primary school, and was beginning to swoon over pop stars on the television, so here was the beginning of another situation requiring careful handling. What girl entering her teens wants her mother tagging along all the time? Claire herself hadn't yet become aware that there might be any problems, but it wouldn't be long.

Claire started high school with a fine mixture of nervousness and excitement which lasted just one day. She settled in with an ease which amazed and delighted us, a tribute to the hard work and sympathetic handling of the staff. The school photographer came on the Monday of the first full week, presumably to take their pictures before they'd had time to mess up their new uniforms, and Claire's photo was lovely. She looked happy and relaxed and thoroughly at home, the complete schoolgirl.

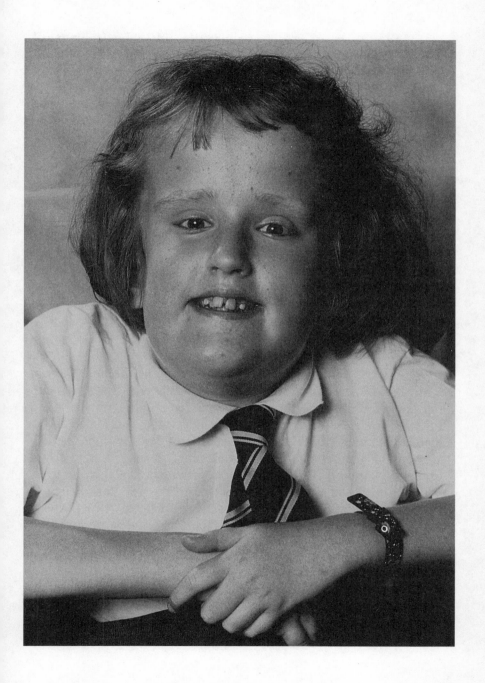

As at primary school she was the only wheelchair pupil, but the other pupils soon got used to her and treated her as part of the crowd. She had her own lift key, which she wore on a ribbon round her neck so that it wouldn't get lost in the depths of her school bag, and the only concession made was that she left each lesson a few minutes early so that she could negotiate the corridors to the next classroom while they were still empty.

Her new helper was a lovely lady, and although she'd never looked after anybody requiring Claire's sort of help before, she soon learnt. I showed her the practical points, Claire trained her in silly stories and witty jokes, and soon the toilet rang with giggles every lunch time. This lady wasn't much bigger than Claire, and was quite unable to lift her, so we devised a new strategy to get Claire in and out of her Skwirrel at tabletop level. Claire worked very hard, but it was quite a strain as she was fighting against gravity all the time. The only good thing was that it also worked at home for getting her in and out of bed. Another case of necessity being the mother of invention!

We had wondered whether Claire would be able to cope with the stricter routine at the high school, with bells marking the end of each lesson and no scope for staying on for a few minutes if she hadn't finished. All her work was typed into a laptop computer provided by the county and sometimes she was slower than the rest of the class at copying things down, especially towards the end of the day when she was getting tired. We needn't have worried. Claire found the regular change of subjects stimulating, and loved nearly all of them. She got very excited over starting French, and her facility with language stood her in good stead. Maggi and Liz had been good at French too, and I dredged up my old O' level vocabulary to converse with them. Poor Elvin was left floundering as he'd never learnt French, and he could see Claire rapidly heading in the same direction as we three, holding secret conversations that he could only guess at.

Homework was another new venture. Elvin linked her laptop to our printer at home, and printed out her day's work which I then stuck in her exercise books. She typed her homework on either the laptop or the big computer, then that was printed off and stuck in. Sometimes she was too tired to type, so I did it at her dictation, mistakes and all. Saturday mornings were reserved for art homework, and she spent hours painstakingly drawing and painting. Her manual dexterity was still below average, but she enjoyed it.

Claire's maths was still her most difficult subject, as hydrocephalus damages certain parts of the brain which deal with spatial relationships. I had noticed that when we were out she had no idea of depth perception; she couldn't tell whether a kerb was a few inches high or like the edge of a cliff, which is all part of the same difficulty. She tried hard though, especially as she liked her maths teacher, who was also her form teacher.

The school was bursting out of its accommodation so a new block of classrooms was being built. They would be ready by Christmas, and would all be rooms for maths. Her class would move into it in the new year, with their maths/form teacher, so progress was watched with interest.

Claire's twelfth birthday came three weeks before Christmas, and around the middle of November she informed me that she wanted to take all the girls in her class to see *Aladdin* at the cinema, then home for tea. This extravagant plan had to be modified as we could only get her and three friends into the car, and it took weeks of soul-searching to choose which three should be invited, she had so many new friends.

Claire's only disappointment that term was the class Christmas outing. They had voted to go by coach to the local ice rink, and she was unable to join them. She couldn't get on the coach, but I could have taken her by car and met them there. Unfortunately the ice rink has a flight of steps to get in, then more down to the ice, and she would only have been able to sit and watch if we'd somehow managed to get her inside. She would have got very cold as well, so she didn't go.

She got rather upset over this. All the primary school outings had been arranged with her access needs in mind, and she had been everywhere with her class. This was the first time she had ever been excluded from anything and she took it hard. I could see that this would happen more and more often in the future, in leisure time if not on official trips, but there was nothing we could do about it.

Claire was getting to the point now where her disability was becoming a nuisance to her. Up to now she had hardly noticed it, as young children don't go to many places by themselves, and she had always been able to do the same things as her friends. Since starting high school her mental horizons had expanded rapidly, and yet her physical limitations were becoming more restricting as her body grew taller and heavier. Claire was only just beginning to be aware of this, but I could see that it could cause quite a lot of distress in the future, even for someone as cheerful and easygoing as she was.

For the very first time since we had started fostering, we would be spending Christmas without anybody else's children in the house. Ann had returned home at the beginning of the summer holidays, and we only had the odd day or two a week of respite children since. In one way this was a good thing, as it let us concentrate single-mindedly on getting Claire settled into the high school, and giving her maximum support during her first term there. On the other hand it meant that we now had virtually no income. We had never earned enough to pay income tax since Elvin left his office job, but we had enough for our needs. Now we were living on Claire's disability allowances, with frequent dips into capital. We had disposed of our second car when we came back from South Africa a year ago, and couldn't really cut down anywhere else, but we managed.

Christmas Day was on a Saturday that year, and Claire didn't break up until the Wednesday before, On the Tuesday we made our annual visit to see the surgeon who had operated on her head and back. As always there was nothing to report, and as always he measured her head and found it still the same as when she was a baby. It didn't look so out of proportion now though, as her body had grown normally.

A bug had been going round the school, probably encouraged by the unseasonably cold weather. Half the children and staff had gone down with a sore throat and bad cold accompanied by severe headaches, and Claire had succumbed a week or two before. She was still having headaches, but her consultant said that her shunt was fine and that no treatment was required beyond paracetamol when necessary, which was a relief.

On the Wednesday, breaking up day, the whole school assembled for a carol service. No hall in the school was big enough to accommodate them all at once so they used the nearby tennis centre. It was a very short walk, but pouring with rain. The caretaker stood halfway there, getting soaked waiting for Claire to come along so that he could help her up the kerb. Such small acts of kindness had been shown to Claire all through her life, by a wide variety of people of all ages; she had the happy, quite unconscious knack of bringing out the best in people. Even the boys who had the potential to be bullies had, in her primary school days, appointed themselves her protectors in the playground, and there was always someone on hand to offer help if she needed it.

Parents were invited to the carol service, so we both went and enjoyed it very much. We were quite amused at the head teacher's admonition at the end: 'Enjoy your Christmas holidays, think what you can do for someone else, and don't forget to wear your correct uniform when you come back.'

After the service the pupils were free to leave, so Claire went shopping on the way home and spent her Christmas money. For years now she had been collecting the model woodland animals called Sylvanian Families and had been coveting the Sylvanian Family bus for a long time. As a £20 note had dropped out of one of her Christmas cards, she was able to supplement her pocket money and buy it. She had amassed a fine collection of Sylvanians bought mostly by herself; we had to keep putting up more shelves to cater for them. Claire had always received the same pocket money as our foster children of the same age, but she didn't fritter it away on sweets so she was always better off. She saved up until she could buy something she really wanted, and, as a bonus hadn't needed any fillings in her teeth – even Maggi and Liz hadn't managed that, and some of our foster children's teeth were in a very poor state when they first came.

That evening Claire was tired. She'd recently had a few bouts of tonsillitis and similar infections which needed antibiotics, and they always pulled her down. In addition she'd just completed her first term at high school and had worked very hard. She had really enjoyed it, but she was definitely ready for a couple of weeks off. Her growth spurt meant that her back had elongated so much that she sometimes had trouble sitting up, as her muscles hadn't had time to grow strong enough to support her all day. Sometimes her heavy head would tip backwards and she couldn't get it up again, and we would have to lie her down and massage her neck and shoulders until she felt better.

Claire spent Wednesday evening relaxing by watching some of her videos of all the *Challenge Anneka* programmes. She especially liked the ones where children were helped, and her all-time favourite was when a refugees' health centre in Malawi was equipped with everything from scratch. This brought together all her interests: there were children, it had medical connections, refugees were helped, and it was in Africa.

Although she must have known this tape off by heart, she never tired of watching it.

Just before she got ready for bed she had another neck ache, and as I tried to relieve it she suddenly said, 'I wish I was dead.' This was so unlike her that I was quite shaken, but I lightly replied, 'That would be lovely for you, but awful for me', and she said no more about it.

On Thursday morning Claire started her Christmas holidays with a leisurely bubble bath and used one of her exotic shampoos – you can always tell girls are growing up when they start fussing with their hair! While her hair dried we sorted through the trinket boxes that had belonged to her two grandmothers. *Blue Peter* had put out an appeal for old jewellery to buy lifeboats, and although we had sent some off there were still odds and ends left. All the valuable items had been shared out among the grandchildren, but there were some beads and old-fashioned costume jewellery left, which Claire enjoyed trying on before packing it all up. At one point she disappeared into her bedroom and came back with her silver christening bracelet, which was now too small for her. This was one of her most precious possessions, but she voluntarily put it with the other things, thinking that a lifeboat radio could be bought from its sale. I didn't disillusion her as to its real worth; as far as she was concerned it was extremely valuable and she was making a great sacrifice.

On Thursday afternoon her best friend from Guides came round, and they played with the Sylvanian collection for hours. We put paste tables down the full length of the living room, and they spread everything out. There was so much that it didn't often all come out together, and they both thoroughly enjoyed themselves.

Friday, Christmas Eve, was a very busy day. Elvin helped Claire with some secret wrapping while I was banished to the

71

kitchen, and then we sent him out while I helped her with his presents. We cleaned the whole house, Claire merrily twirling round the kitchen with a wet mop until her arm ached. We went to the village to post the *Blue Peter* parcel and get some last minute shopping, and watched the weather forecasts with great excitement as snow was promised. Claire wanted to stay up late to watch some special television programmes, so she went to have a lie-down before tea, and actually went to sleep for half an hour.

After tea she mixed the stuffing for the turkey, made chocolate butter icing and decorated a Swiss roll as a Christmas log, and helped to prepare the vegetables and side dishes. I didn't want to spend Christmas Day in the kitchen, so we did as much as possible the night before. Elvin's Dad would be coming over for Christmas dinner, Maggi would come on Sunday and Liz on Monday, so we needed quite a lot of food even though we were such a small family now.

Very late in the evening, just as Claire was getting ready for bed, her previous school helper and her husband called in, bearing gifts. These were put under the tree, and Claire presented them with a bowl of daffodils she had planted at half-term. Their baby was due in about another two months, and Claire had to inspect the bump and have a full progress report. By the time we had watched our programmes and finally got Claire ready for bed it was well after ten, so she asked if she could carry out our Christmas Eve ceremony in bed. Every year since Maggi was a baby we have sung carols by candlelight on Christmas Eve, and then the children have gone to bed and hung up their stockings by candlelight. As the number of children increased we had to limit the carols to one each, or it would have gone on for ever, so Claire was very thrilled to be allowed a bonus choice as the only child present.

As I settled her into her sleeping position and helped her to adjust her Christmas stocking Elvin silently arranged the presents under the tree; our stairs were too creaky to have allowed us to do it secretly after she was in bed!

The high school had broken up so late that there were only two full days of holidays before Christmas, but Claire enjoyed them both to the hilt. We remarked, as we went to bed, that she had had two completely perfect days.

8

Christmas alone

As soon as Claire was settled we went to bed, but I stayed awake to creep in with her full stocking once she was asleep. I must have dozed off as it was half-past midnight when I heard her moaning. I thought she must have wind – she'd been scraping bowls and nibbling all evening – so I tried to ignore it for a while. I didn't really want to get out of my warm bed; the forecast was for minus six that night and I was nice and cosy.

However, she didn't settle, so I thought I'd better go down as she may have felt sick. When I went into her bedroom Claire put her head up and said, 'I haven't slept a wink!' She sounded mortally offended, and I told her that was what came of having granny naps in the afternoon!

Claire seemed to have a frog in her throat, and as it's difficult to cough when lying on your tummy, I asked her if she'd like to sit up for a minute. She couldn't do this by herself, as the bedclothes hampered her movements, so I turned her over and sat her up. The frog in her throat was very bad and she didn't seem able to cough; in fact her breathing was so poor I thought she'd better have the doctor. I shouted for Elvin, who'd remained comfortably in bed, and he came down to 'phone. At that moment Claire collapsed against my arm, turned blue, and stopped breathing altogether.

I shook her and thumped frantically on her chest, shouting, 'Breathe! Breathe!' but there was no response. Elvin, not having yet reached the doctor, changed to a 999 call for an ambulance. I realised it was no good just waiting for them to arrive. I would have to give Claire the kiss of life to keep her going until they came.

It is one thing to do a first aid course in a church hall, in quite a light-hearted atmosphere among friends, joking as you take turns puffing into a plastic dummy. It is quite another thing to be suddenly faced with the need to do it for real on your own child, in the middle of the night. My knees had turned to jelly, and I had to lean on Claire's bed for support as I laid her down with a silent prayer for help and started breathing into her. I don't panic easily, but I came within striking distance of it then. A little voice somewhere in the back of my brain was quoting, 'Tilt the head back, pinch the nose, breathe steadily, watch for the chest to rise.' It was years since the first aid course, but I followed the instructions – apart perhaps from the 'breathe steadily' bit – and was almost overcome with relief when Claire started breathing again. It was very faltering at first, and I was doing alternate breaths for her for a time, but she gradually established a steady rhythm and became semi-conscious.

Elvin had flung on some clothes and ran to the end of our close to direct the ambulance, and I turned Claire on to her side and made reassuring noises. Her nails were still blue, and she obviously needed some oxygen, but she was able to respond when I spoke to her. When the ambulance arrived the paramedics gave her oxygen and arranged for a police escort, and we were whisked off to our local casualty department. I travelled in the ambulance with Claire; Elvin followed in our car with some clothes for me (I was in my nightie and dressing gown) and Claire's filled Christmas stocking.

The casualty staff were waiting for us, and tried to establish what had happened. Had she been eating sweets in bed and choked? Had she had a fit? Had she been sick and breathed some of it in? The answer to all these questions was 'No', but different people kept coming and asking them over and over again. They also wanted Claire's hospital records, but she didn't have any as she'd only been in the children's special hospital for the operations, never in this local one through illness. They kept her on oxygen, with the concentration gradually reducing, and sent her for a chest X-ray, which was clear. Eventually they decided that she must have choked on some phlegm in her throat, and although the episode was now over she would have to stay in for observation.

Claire was put to bed in the children's ward, virtually empty because it was Christmas. A nurse made us a very welcome cup of tea, and we relaxed. The sister explained that Claire would have to stay for twenty-four hours, and we made plans to bring the Skwirrel in after breakfast. She was obviously tired, but different people still kept coming to ask questions – they had no medical history – and to take various observations of her. Claire was nearly off the oxygen by now – the mask lay near her face rather than on it, and was at the lowest concentration. I took advantage of a quiet moment to get dressed, then another doctor arrived to ask if Claire was having chest pains. I asked her, 'Where does it hurt?' and she clearly replied, 'Nowhere.' The doctor went away, and nobody came for a while, so I settled Claire down on her tummy to sleep. It was about 5am. I sat next to the bed watching Claire and going over the last few hours. My knees ached from the trembling they had done earlier, and I was still too het up to relax enough to doze. I watched Claire's breathing – she had finally gone to sleep – and suddenly realised that it was stopping again.

The medical staff flocked around instantly, and Elvin and I were banished to the playroom round the corner. It was 5.45am on Christmas morning, but we didn't feel very Christmassy. The doctor who had asked about chest pains appeared and completely floored us by asking how hard we wanted them to try to resuscitate Claire. Until then we had no idea that her situation was serious; they had given us the impression that the crisis was over. Now they were suddenly talking of ventilators and death, and we were stunned. When the doctor left us, saying we didn't have to give an immediate answer, we just looked at each other. We held hands and sat in silence, too dazed with shock to say much. I could only pray wordlessly, 'Lord, don't let her suffer', over and over again.

It seemed a very long time before they let us back into the ward, and things were very different now. Claire was lying against pillows on her back with her head to one side, with the oxygen mask back on. She was unconscious, but not blue. She had a drip up, and several monitors surrounding her. Staff were bustling about, but she was unaware of it all.

Elvin 'phoned our minister, who promptly left his family and came to the hospital to support us. He also tried to 'phone Maggi and Liz, but they had both been out on Christmas Eve and he couldn't get an answer.

The same doctor came back and explained that there was no hope for Claire. They now thought she had suffered a pulmonary embolism, and it was too severe for treatment. She had started to bleed from her lungs, and needed frequent suction to clear her throat. A portable X-ray machine was brought to her bed, and this now showed that her lungs were completely cloudy, where only hours before they had been clear.

Elvin and I were grief-stricken, yet accepted that Claire's life was over. We stood together holding hands in the playroom and gave her back to God and his care, and waited for the end.

At about nine o'clock the chief paediatrician came and the junior doctor went off duty. He asked all the questions again, examined Claire and looked at the X-rays, then decided that he would pull out all the stops to give her a chance, because there was no brain damage. He wasn't convinced it was an embolism; he thought it might be a massive infection.

We had resigned ourselves to inevitable death, but now there was a sudden spark of hope. The doctor wanted Claire in intensive care at a children's hospital, and started 'phoning round for a place. 'Her' hospital had no vacancies, which was disappointing as all her records were there and it was familiar ground. He eventually found a bed at the hospital Penny had been in, but they were already committed to collecting another child. When that one had been admitted and stabilised they would come for Claire, probably just after lunch.

Elvin started ringing everybody again with this update, but still couldn't contact Maggi or Liz. Our minister had to leave us to take his morning service, and we sat with Claire. Once the paediatric intensive care bed was organised Elvin went home to get a case for me. I would be staying with Claire and needed spare clothes and toiletries for both of us, some money and a few of Claire's favourite books to read to her once she was well enough.

It didn't need medical training to see that Claire was obviously getting worse. The alarms on her monitors were going off at increasingly short intervals, the blood was bubbling out of her mouth more and more, and extra drips were being put up and injections given. The only crumb of comfort was that she was still unconscious and so totally unaware of it.

The doctor decided to take Claire up to intensive care to keep her going until the specialist team arrived, so we had a silent rush through the corridors. A crowd of doctors and nurses pushed the bed along rapidly, while holding drips and monitors, and one pumped an air bag as he ran. I hurried along behind, glancing through the large windows to see that it was snowing heavily. The forecasters had got it right, and I felt a pang of regret that Claire was missing it. It was rather ridiculous in the face of everything else that was happening, but one of the last things Claire had said as she went to bed – could it have only been so few hours ago? – was, 'Do you think it will *really* snow tomorrow?' She had been so excited at the prospect.

Claire's bed was whisked into intensive care and the doors swung shut in my face. I had to wait alone in a tiny windowless room while they stabilised her, and the minutes dragged past endlessly. I was there about an hour before the doctor came out. He told me sorrowfully that Claire was losing the battle, and asked what I wanted to do. I asked him to 'phone Elvin and tell him to come back, and said I wanted to hold Claire. He left me alone again, choked with hot sobs of grief, until a nurse came to escort me into intensive care.

By now I had myself under control, however precariously, and was able to speak to the nurse looking after Claire. I lay on the bed alongside her and took her in my arms, but something indefinable was missing. She was still attached to drips and monitors, a ventilator was breathing for her, she looked the same and yet wasn't the same. I said to the nurse, 'She's not here, is she?' and she shook her head, indicating the array of monitors behind the bed and saying, 'The output has been flat for some time.' Claire, so full of life, and love and laughter, was dead.

I asked the nurse to remove all the wires and needles, but to leave the ventilator on. I thought it would be a shade less distressing for Elvin if Claire at least appeared to be breathing when he arrived. He isn't as comfortable with medical things as I am, and I tried to soften the impact a little. He arrived very shortly, and the nurse left us alone with Claire. We both cried, and yet there was an element of pure joy in our sorrow, like a shaft of sunlight in a huge dark cave. Claire was no longer disabled! She had joined Penny in heaven, free from the shackles of her disabled body.

This was only a very small part of it though. Our main feelings were of grief and shock; it had all been so sudden.

Claire was still on the ventilator, and we asked the nurse to turn it off. I have read of the agonies people have gone through in making this decision, yet part of me stood back in surprise at how easy it was. Claire was so obviously dead, for all she appeared to be breathing, that there was no pain at all in asking for it to be disconnected. She now lay in bed as if asleep, looking her usual self apart from being on her back. I combed her hair, which had got thoroughly messed up during the resuscitation attempts, and she looked absolutely calm and peaceful.

Elvin had finally managed to contact Maggi while he had been at home, and she now arrived. Of course she only knew that Claire was very ill, and was devastated to find that she had just died. We had our hands full trying to calm her. She and Claire had spoken on the 'phone the evening before, a happy conversation looking forward to Maggi's planned visit on Boxing Day, but they hadn't seen each other for a few weeks, and Maggi was quite overcome.

After a little while I remembered Claire's wish that her 'bits' be used when she no longer needed them, and asked about organ donation. Unfortunately the manner of her death meant that her internal organs couldn't be used, but her corneas weren't damaged and arrangements were made for them to be collected.

A little later Maggi left, deeply distressed, and was taken home by the friend who had brought her. The doctor came to speak to us, offering condolences and explaining that there would have to be a post mortem before he could issue a death certificate, as he wasn't sure what had caused Claire's death. The coroner would not be back at work until Tuesday, so it would probably be the end of the week before we knew.

At about three o'clock on Christmas afternoon Elvin and I left the hospital and drove home. We hardly spoke. There didn't seem to be words for how we felt.   When we opened the front door we were confronted by the Christmas tree, with piles of unopened presents beneath it, which was a very poignant moment. The house was cold and silent; mechanically we lit the fire and made a cup of tea.

I rang my sister in South Africa and finally made contact with Liz. Of course they both thought we were just 'phoning with Christmas greetings and had to be cruelly disillusioned. After the first shock they were both full of questions, but we were totally unable to give any answers.

Once we had run out of things to do we could only hold each other and weep. It was Christmas alone indeed.

9

Not the end but the beginning

The next few days were spent in a haze of shock. Because it was Christmas people were spending time with their families and not meeting each other at schools, church or shops as usual, so news of Claire's death spread very slowly at first. Many of our friends had been at the Christmas morning service, and had heard our minister announce Claire's sudden illness, and then they had gone away for the rest of the holiday. Once they returned they 'phoned us for news, so we were having to go over it all again and again. Of course they all wanted to know the cause of her death, but we still didn't know.

People started coming to see us, loving and caring friends who had shared our joy in Claire and now shared our grief at the sudden separation. Rather than keep repeating what had happened at the hospital, I gave them a letter to read which explained it all. This was a letter I had written to my sister which fully described what had happened – I couldn't give her all the details over the phone – and Elvin had photocopied it. It had been written in the early hours of Boxing Day, when I had been unable to sleep.

We had gone to bed at about 9pm on Christmas Day, worn out after more than thirty-one hours without sleep and the most harrowing experience of our lives. We had eventually slept from sheer exhaustion, but 3am found us downstairs again. It seemed so odd to have lights on and to be able to talk in normal voices in the middle of the night; we hadn't been alone in the house at night since Maggi was born. We made the inevitable cup of tea, then I wrote the letter to South Africa.

The next night I woke again in the small hours, but this time my head was full of a poem. I didn't consciously write it, I just woke up and it was there. Not having paper and pencil in the bedroom, I went downstairs to write it down, as I didn't want to lose it. It wasn't until I had written it down and read it several times that the meaning really hit me.

'Not the end but the beginning'

Before my birth I was alive
But restricted.
Then she had to part from me
And it was painful for her.

But for me it was the beginning of my new life
Which has far surpassed anything
I could have thought of in the womb.

Before my death I was alive
But restricted.
Now you have to part from me
And it is painful for you.

But for me it is the beginning of my new life
Which is far surpassing anything
I could have thought of in my time.

Then there came a verse from the Bible – 'No eye has seen, nor ear has heard, no mind has conceived, what God has prepared for those who love him.'

As I sat and re-read these lines over and over again, a great joy welled up within me. At that moment I learnt the difference between joy and happiness. We were desperately unhappy – losing a much loved child is the worst that can happen to a parent. I am not normally a weepy type (in fact I usually conceal my emotions so well that my sister once commented that I wasn't born, but quarried) but both my nose and eyes were red and sore from repeated bouts of crying.

My thoughts went back to what I had said to Claire on the subject of her death three days ago – 'It would be lovely for you but awful for me.' Although I had said that off the top of my head without much thought its truth was now very apparent.

At the same time I was now so delighted for Claire's sake that the two were equal and opposite, leaving me balanced in the middle. I had a most curious and unbelievable sense of calm, which I can only suppose is what the Bible means when it speaks of 'the peace which passes understanding'.

As more and more visitors came to the house, I was able to share the poem with them and comfort them, and we were able to tell many people what God had done for Claire when she was a baby.

It also became very clear that God had been at work now, too. The more we thought about it, the more we realised that her death had been another example of God's perfect timing. Claire had enjoyed a very happy childhood, despite not being able to walk. In fact she had done more things and been to more places than many able-bodied children, and lived life to the full. I had no regrets at all about her life so far, none of the painful 'if onlys' that are so often present when a loved one dies. I had wished that the surgeons could have operated on her head as soon as it started to enlarge, but that was beyond my control.

I had seen problems ahead for Claire as a teenager, and the cut-off point had come just as these were showing signs of beginning. All my worries and concerns for her, both physical and emotional, were now ended. She could now walk, run, dance – someone unctuously said, 'She's at peace now' – but I flatly disagreed. She and Penny were more likely to be racing round at ninety miles an hour, tripping everybody up!

As she heard Bible stories, and especially as she became intimately acquainted with Joseph and Noah through the musical productions, Claire often came up with detailed questions which weren't answered in the Bible narrative. Her response was always, 'Never mind, I can ask them when I see them in heaven.'

She was also actively looking forward to being reunited with Penny and three of her grandparents, and had worked out for herself that she would be able to walk when she got there.

For Claire, heaven was a real and tangible place, as real and tangible as London, another place she had heard a lot about and looked forward to seeing one day. There was nothing in the least morbid about all this. Claire was enthusiastic in all her plans for the future. She wanted to visit London and see the crown jewels, she wanted to explore the ancient remains in York, she wanted to go to EuroDisney when her French was more extensive, and she wanted to see her friends in heaven. She talked about all these places with equal enthusiasm, and they were all eagerly anticipated.

On one of his visits our minister asked what I thought of it being Christmas Day when Claire died. I hadn't really thought about it before, but one of Claire's favourite new Christmas songs says, 'Heaven invites you to a party, to celebrate the birth of the Son.' She had responded to the invitation and gone to the party! She had hung up her stocking on Christmas Eve with all due excitement and pleasurable anticipation, and woken up in heaven. What a way to go!

We still didn't know exactly why Claire had died, until the coroner rang late on Thursday morning. To our complete surprise he told us it had been the grown-up equivalent of a cot death, called 'adult respiratory distress syndrome'. We had never heard of such a thing, but he explained that he had seen six cases in his area over the last ten years, one of them being a fit young soldier in our village. It was nothing to do with her disability, it could happen to anybody. Once we had digested this surprising information there were more aspects of Claire's death to thank God for. If I hadn't heard her in the night we would have found her dead in bed the next morning, which would have been a far greater shock than it was already. Because she died in hospital we were spared police involvement and an inquest, for which we were very grateful.

We belong to our local spina bifida society, and several of their young adult members have died of kidney failure over the last few years. This involved weeks in hospital, with long, drawn-out distress for both the patient and the family. We had already been through a terminal illness with Penny, and it would have been agonisingly heartbreaking to have to go through another such experience with Claire.

There is nothing worse for parents than to watch their child suffer. When I had been in hospital with Claire for her operations I had often talked with other mums, and very often they had said, 'I wish it could be me.' We knew that Claire hadn't had any pain – the last thing she had said was that it didn't hurt, when the doctor had asked about chest pains. Claire still had a very low pain threshold, so she couldn't have had any discomfort at all when she said it didn't hurt. She had then drifted comfortably off to sleep, and never woken up again. She had suffered no distress through all the subsequent medical attention as she was unconscious, and we were very thankful.

Now that we had a death certificate we could go ahead and organise Claire's funeral, which was also to be a thanksgiving service for her life. With so many bank holidays over Christmas and the New Year, combined with the delay for the post mortem, there was over a fortnight between her death and the funeral, but that was a good thing as it meant that we were into the new school term, and her friends would be able to come.

As we had talked to various people about Claire's life, we had shown them photographs of her, and we now mounted a selection of these on to display boards and put them up in the foyer of the church, together with captions explaining how she had been expected to be a cabbage but that God had intervened. They made a marvellous collection of action photographs, from baby snaps through swimming, archery, horse riding, cooking, drama, gardening, arts and crafts to her twelfth birthday, just three weeks before her death. They included her high spots of being enrolled in Brownies and Guides, and the wedding at which she was bridesmaid, her adoption; and the trip to South Africa. The Turbo and the Skwirrel were featured, and the centre piece was a small wall hanging Claire had recently made in Junior Church. The word 'JOY' topped a leaping figure with arms upraised, skipping over sunlit hills. This seemed a fitting tribute to Claire's present condition, and the whole display evoked her love of life and vibrant personality.

The church is in the centre of the village and the foyer is open all day, so hundreds of people saw the photographs. We wanted to share with them our sense of wonder at what this 'cabbage' had achieved, our gratitude at being part of it, and our joy that she was now running around in heaven, perfectly whole.

We expected that a lot of people would want to come to Claire's funeral and express their sympathy by giving something. As at Penny's service, we decided to have family flowers only, and invite other friends to make a donation. In Penny's case we had sent the money to buy floating toys for her school's new hydrotherapy pool, so now we had to decide on another suitable recipient. We wanted to support something that Claire herself had been interested in, but her interests were so wide-ranging that they were difficult to narrow down to a single one. Eventually we had a brainwave – the *Challenge Anneka* project in Malawi that Claire had loved so much.

Although the tape had been played time and time again, we had never taken much notice of who had set the challenge, so we had to watch it again to find out. We found the tape halfway through the programme; it was the last one Claire had played. We discovered that it was done through Christian Aid, so we looked in the 'phone book for them. We didn't want to 'phone long distance to London, so looked in the directory for our nearest large city, and were pleased to find that Christian Aid had an office there. Unfortunately they told us that the Malawi project was completed, which rather disappointed us. We asked if they had anything similiar, involving children in Africa, and although the lady didn't know immediately she promised to find out and ring us back.

When she rang again it was to ask if a project in South Africa would be all right. Of course we agreed, so she explained that it was for street children in Cape Town. We were overjoyed by the coincidence (or was it be another of God's incidents?) – we hadn't mentioned that Claire had been to Cape Town when we originally told her why we wanted to send some money.

The project was called Molo Songololo, which took us a while to learn to pronounce. The people involved produce a regular magazine for children of all races, which aims to amuse, educate and break down barriers. They had recently opened a shelter for street children, and needed money to make a permanent home for them. Molo Songololo means 'hello centipede' in the African language Xhosa, and we gathered that it represented a lot of children's feet all moving in the same direction. Claire had keenly supported a project for street children in Columbia, run by her previous Sunday School, and as she had actually been to Cape Town we thought Christian Aid had come up with the ideal proposal.

About two hundred people came to Claire's funeral, so many that they overflowed into the foyer. Many of her school friends came, and I think they quite enjoyed it. The tone of the service was happy and thankful, with plenty of singing, although of course there was also a strong current of sadness at her sudden loss. A lot of people there had never been to a funeral service before, and were rather dreading it, but from the comments afterwards I think they were pleasantly surprised. Claire's photographs were the centre of a lot of interest, and we were very grateful for so many donations for Molo Songololo that we were able to send off well over £1,000 to Christian Aid.

Two other agreeable plans were made to honour Claire's memory. Her head teacher came to see us and explained that some money had been allocated for landscaping around the new maths block, and she proposed that there should be a rose garden there, dedicated to Claire's memory. We thought this was a charming idea, and very suitable in view of her name.

Claire's Guide leader had a similiar suggestion. The Guides bought a spring flowering tree in Claire's memory and planted it in the centre of the church garden. We were invited to the tree-planting ceremony, and I commented that I felt like the Queen as I ceremoniously shovelled in a spadeful of earth with the minister and all the Guides looking on.

10

Next

After Claire had been buried with Penny, and Maggi and Liz had returned home, we were left with nothing to do. The flow of sympathetic visitors dwindled, the house was soon put in apple-pie order – and with no children in the house, it stayed that way.

We decided to accept my sister's invitation to visit her again. This time we would stay for two months so that we could look after things while they had a holiday. We thought we might as well do nothing there as at home (the cost of living was actually less there) and we had fallen in love with South Africa when we went the first time. Elvin was a bit nervous about leaving our house empty for so long so we packed our irreplaceable videos and tapes and farmed small boxes out around our friends, then left England on 1st March.

Although we had got over the first shock of Claire's sudden death, and were now able to sleep and eat normally again, we found that tears were triggered by the most unpredictable things. When we arrived at the airport I unexpectedly had to vanish twice into the Ladies to mop up, because Claire had been with us last time we came. This feeling followed me through all the early part of the holiday, as Claire had previously been with us everywhere we went. Later on we explored other places and I felt better.

Because my sister lives within striking distance of Cape Town we had the immense satisfaction of being able to visit Molo Songololo. We were acutely aware of another chain of

91

'coincidence' – the minister of the church we attended as holiday visitors had (quite unknown to us) previously had a church in that area, and so knew it intimately. He and his wife offered to take us, which greatly simplified the travel arrangements. As an unexpected bonus we discovered that they had just returned from three years in the UK working at another church in our circuit, and they had actually met our minister!

We went first to the Molo Songololo offices, where the magazine is produced, and met the staff. Claire's display of photographs went with us; when they were taken down from the church foyer I had put them into a large photo album, together with captions. We showed them these, and explained about Claire's sudden death and the reason why they were receiving 'her' money. They said they might do an article about her in the Molo magazine, and asked us to organise some comments from her school friends.

There were back numbers of the Molo magazine for sale, so we were able to buy some to take home with us, and also some posters they produce on 'The Rights of the Child'. Children are often very much second class citizens in the third world, and Molo Songololo is pushing for the recognition of basic rights which we take for granted.

After visiting the office we were taken to the street children's shelter some miles away. This was once a council depot in the first township ever built in the Cape Town area. It had bays for the storage of sand, cement and gravel, with offices, toilets and a kitchen. The whole building was surrounded by a narrow yard enclosed with a high wall and secure gates. Ten years ago the council had left, and it had stood empty ever since. As well as emptying it, they had pulled out all the electrical fittings. Wires protruded from the walls where switches had once been, and the ceilings were badly damaged in places where light fittings had been crudely pulled away. Although there was still water there were only three toilets and one (cold) shower that worked.

This was 'home' for twenty-five boys, a mere drop in the ocean compared with the five or six hundred estimated to live on the streets of Cape Town. Most of them were at school when we visited, but a dozen or so were being taught in a large room before they progressed to the local schools. The teacher had to beg her materials from local stationers, but the boys were keen to learn as they realised that education was the only way out of their poverty trap. All their lessons were done in three languages – Xhosa, Afrikaans and English. The windows were small so the room was gloomy despite the bright African sunshine, and at night they only had candlelight. On Friday afternoons they had a treat – the lady next door ran an extension lead over the wall and they watched two hours of television. The kitchen couldn't be used without electricity, and was in a state of disrepair.

We were so glad we had been able to send some money, although they told us about another problem. The council would only give them a three months' lease, and they had to apply to renew it after that time. They could have been forced to leave at any time, so there was no point in spending any money on the building. At the end of our holiday, two days before we flew home, we 'phoned Molo for the latest update and were delighted to hear that a council official had just visited the shelter and said they could have the building. They were waiting to have this confirmed in writing, then they could go ahead and make the necessary repairs and improvements.

We flew home on South Africa's first all-races Election Day, and found a very surprising invitation awaiting us. We were invited to the High School for the official opening of the 'Claire Rose Mathematics Suite' – they had named the whole new block after her!

The ceremony was a grand formal affair, with the Director of Education for the county unveiling a plaque, speeches (including one from Elvin in which he gave thanks for Claire's life and dedicated the building and the rose garden to her memory) and excellent music and food provided by the pupils. The weather was fine enough for the proceedings to be held in the rose garden outside, which included a large sunny paved area with seats. The school photo Claire had had taken at the beginning of term was mounted above the plaque with these words:

> Claire was an extremely brave girl who, despite suffering from severe spina bifida, overcame her physical handicaps to attend normal primary school. In September 1993, along with her friends, she transferred to the High School.
> Having enjoyed a very happy first term she sadly died, suddenly and without pain, on Christmas Day. Claire taught us all a great deal. Her smile was captivating and her courage was inspiring. She would have moved into a new form base in the Mathematics block in January 1994 and it is a fitting tribute that the suite be named after her.

We felt very honoured that they had thought so much of Claire; after all, she had only been there for one term. On another occasion we showed her class the slides and photos we had taken at Molo Songololo, and left the magazines for them to read. We also showed them to her former primary school, and both schools decided to maintain a link through Christian Aid, supporting the street children as an ongoing tribute to Claire.

Claire's helper's baby was born on the day we left for South Africa – a little boy called Daniel – and we went to his christening on our first Sunday back. We were delighted to meet him at last, although I had a tiny sad thought about how much Claire would have loved him.

Once all this flurry of excitement was over, and we had retrieved our possessions and settled in at home again, we were faced with the question of what to do with ourselves.

Our social worker keeps telling us that we are 'a valuable resource', but she can't produce any more children for us. There are plenty who need respite care at weekends, but this is hardly a full-time job and we can't live indefinitely with virtually no income.

We did wonder if God had 'cleared the decks' so that we could have a change of direction, but so far nothing has presented itself. If we had found something to do in South Africa we would have seriously considered moving there; Maggi and Liz are now independent young women with their own lives to lead and although we frequently keep in touch by 'phone, it could easily be by letters. However, nothing materialised there, so we remain English Roses rather than tropical blooms.

Elvin has looked for a job around here, but middle-aged men can't just walk into employment in the present economic climate. Besides, we have always worked well as a team, and would prefer to do something together. I don't suppose that there are any statistics about the number of couples who continue to be friends after twenty-seven years of marriage, but we still enjoy each other's company!

As the old hymn puts it:

We don't know what the future holds
But we know Who holds the future.

The answer to the question 'What next?' remains 'Wait and see!'

Postscript

Great is thy faithfulness

It is now three years since Claire's death, and the Christmas decorations are up again. So much has happened that I need to bring the story up to date.

I was reading the local paper just two weeks after writing Claire's story, and saw an advertisement for a 'Link Club Co-ordinator'. Link Clubs cover the gap between children finishing school and parents coming home from work. They also run all day during school holidays, and a new one was being set up in a nearby school. I applied and got the job! I was rather surprised as I thought I would be considered too old, but there was little time for cold feet as the club opened in September and the interviews weren't held until mid-August.

We started with nine children, and have now (in our third year) built up to our maximum of twenty-four each night, and thirty in the holidays; helped by some very able assistant leaders. I have had to pass a minibus driving test as we collect the children from their schools, which quite impressed Maggi and Liz. Their friends' parents are quietly sliding into middle age, and here am I starting a new career!

During term time I have my mornings free, which gives me ample time to potter around the house, then I go into school at lunchtime. Club closes at 6 pm, so there is still enough evening left to do a bit of gardening (in the summer) or go to choir practice and other meetings. The job feels tailor-made for me, and I have no doubt that it was – it didn't exist until just the time I needed it!

Elvin too has been busy as he has been appointed as a Lay Pastoral Assistant. Although it is not a paid job, he is doing what he loves – visiting people in their homes. He also spends hours at his computer doing posters for the church noticeboard, the weekly notice sheet and the monthly church newsletter.

At around the same time as Elvin's appointment – on Bonfire Night – Beth moved in with us. She had been for respite care a couple of times, but home circumstances meant that she needed to move. She had many health problems, and was very small for her age of six and a half. She was so frail that she had to lean on every lamp-post for a rest even on the shortest walk. Many operations had kept her in hospital for long periods, and she went to a special school where there were nurses on hand to care for her during the day. Beth stayed on at the same school, but Elvin brought her to Link Club afterwards so that she had a chance to mix with ordinary children. At first she was a real fish out of water, but she gradually learnt to be part of the group. Her health has improved out of all recognition; she has grown a lot and become strong and sturdy, and has now moved on to one of the local primary schools. Her own summary of the situation is, 'I *used* to be disabled.'

We have stayed in touch with Christian Aid, and Claire was featured in their Life Stories magazine under the title 'Claire's Legacy of Hope'. Molo Songololo also carried an article about her, with a photograph and contributions from two of her school friends.

To our great surprise we were invited to the BBC's studios to take part in the live Radio Four programme *Sunday*. This was near Christmas, when Christmas Eve fell on a Sunday. We had to get up at an unearthly hour in the pitch dark to be at the studios for 8am, where we were offered coffee and mince pies! Beth came with us, and was looked after in another room while we went into the sound-proofed studio. We had to pass through the control room, all switches and dials, which Elvin found fascinating as he does a lot of recording himself. I was too nervous to be natural, but we took part in an interesting discussion with Colin Morris (in bright red socks and no shoes!) a parish priest, and a lady from the Samaritans. Then we had to rush back as I was producing the children's nativity play at our 9.45am service.

Mercifully, life isn't always so rushed and exciting. We have long periods of 'the daily round and common task', when the daily and weekly routines flow along quietly. Beth is a bubbly chatterbox who keeps us on our toes, and we have another girl of the same age who comes for respite care every other weekend.

We are constantly aware of God's care and provision for us. Was it just coincidence that the same day our big estate car – now 10 years old – was pronounced unable to pass her next MOT test, there 'just happened' to be an ex-demonstration Fiesta sitting on the garage forecourt, thirteen months old and with only 1,867 miles on the clock? It was exactly the price we could afford, and was even the colour we prefer for cars – white.

We have just returned from our third holiday in South Africa. As a 'working woman' I only had enough holiday allowance to go for three weeks, but it was well worth it. It was the first time Beth had flown, and she enjoyed every minute of the holiday, so much that she refused to come home and had to be bribed back to the airport with little gifts from the friends she had made.

It has been a real joy to watch her progress over the two years that she has been with us. Her health is now established, and she merges with the crowd at Club. She has coped remarkably well with the change from her sheltered special school to the rough-and-tumble of normal primary school, and she now considers herself an ordinary child – quite a transformation.

And what of the future? The hymn we chose to sing at our wedding, nearly thirty years ago now, sums it up neatly:

> Great is thy faithfulness! Great is thy faithfulness!
> Morning by morning new mercies I see;
> All I have needed thy hand has provided:
> Great is thy faithfulness, Lord, unto me.

Printed by Clifford Frost Limited, Lyon Road, Windsor Avenue, Wimbledon, London SW19 2SE